PRAISE FOR
A SELF-CARE GUIDE

This is the most useful resource I have come across in the art therapy field! It is so meaningful to have mindfulness exercises and directives that work together, ones that are thoughtful and not just pencil and paper directives! As someone who is just starting out it is so important to have this kind of guidance for the flow of meaningful directives. It feels like you wrote this for me!

— ALISHA D'SOUZA, ART THERAPY STUDENT,
TORONTO ART THERAPY INSTITUTE

I so loved this book! I stayed up into the wee hours of morning to finish reading it! Something I haven't done in quite a long time! I really enjoyed this book. I especially liked how each activity began with an intention. Focusing on the breath, guiding the individual to a spiritual space before beginning. This is such a beautiful practice.

— LINDA GIBBS, EXPRESSIVE ARTS THERAPIST

I enjoyed this book very much and loved how it is arranged! This book features excellent, unique meditations and art therapy exercises. Some of the prompts use music, nature, photos, and, of course, art materials. The meditations and exercises help readers engage in self-care that facilitates grounding and helping people become centered.

— MERA RASTOGI, PHD, ATR+BC, ART THERAPY
PROFESSOR AT UNIVERSITY OF CINCINNATI
CLERMONT COLLEGE

I especially liked the "mindful" approach to each activity which enabled me to "savor", even "luxuriate" in the process. As a Therapeutic Movement Facilitator, we need these reminders every so often. I will be incorporating these activities into my workshops!

— HATHER JOANNE MALOTO, THERAPEUTIC
MOVEMENT FACILITATOR, PHILIPPINES

This is a one-of-a-kind work of art. It is a brilliant guide for an expressive arts practitioner like me who has a hectic schedule. This book gave me an easy guide with all of the flow I needed. Thank you for sharing this gift. Continue to work on more books that will help us expressive arts practitioners across the globe!

— DR. CHERRY MAY ROTAS- PALACIO, FOUNDER
SELF-CARE PROJECT 2030, MENTAL HEALTH
PROFESSIONAL, PHILIPPINES

THE ART THERAPY WAY: A SELF-CARE GUIDE

30 MINUTE ART THERAPY ACTIVITIES TO CALM
ANXIETY, IMPROVE MOOD, DE-STRESS, AND
CONNECT TO YOUR INNER VOICE

KENDYL ARDEN

The Art Therapy Way: A Self-Care Guide

30 minute art therapy activities to calm anxiety, improve mood, de-stress, and connect to your inner voice

Kendyl Arden

CONTENTS

INTRODUCTION

"This is hard, but I can do hard things."

These were the words I spoke to myself, over and over again for a year, as I struggled to make it through the hardest season of my life: when I lost the most important person to me. As the trauma and pain waged war in my body and mind I constantly felt as though I was gasping for air. The weight of anxiety and grief suffocated me and I was drowning under the waves of words I was unable to speak, so I turned to art to process and to grieve.

I found that it was in those moments that art gave a voice to my heartache within me and overtime I wasn't drowning, but instead I was swimming. Art was like this breath that brought me up above the waves, even if it was only for a moment.

Art was medicine.

Art was healing.

When the world around me did not make sense, art helped me to bring meaning and beauty into dark spaces.

And this is why I wrote this book.

In 2019 I moved to Kathmandu, Nepal to help with an art therapy program for children that were survivors of sex trafficking. This was the first time, apart from my own life, that I saw the healing that art can bring to others. I saw survivors be brought to tears as they shared the burdens they were holding through making art, and as they shared they began walking in freedom, away from shame and darkness. When I moved home to the states I enrolled in an art therapy graduate program, as I was completely moved by my experience in Nepal as well as my personal one. Currently, I am an art therapist and have seen over and over again how art speaks when words alone are not enough.

With that, this book is for those who are struggling. It is for those who want to develop a creative outlet and connect to their inner voice. It is for those who are looking for healing, rest, comfort, relief, and hope. You do not have to be an artist to create meaningful art, or to partake in any of these activities. This book is about the process of art making, not the product, and it is about connecting with your voice more than creating something aesthetically pleasing. And finally, this book is **NOT** a replacement for therapy, and this statement is not to be overlooked. **It is merely a self care resource and uses art as a therapeutic outlet.** Please seek out help if you know that you need therapeutic support.

WHAT IS ART THERAPY

"The task of therapy is not to eliminate suffering, but to give a voice to it, to find a form in which it can be expressed."
-Stephen K. Levine

Art therapy is a clinical practice that uses the creative process in psychotherapy to improve well-being. The process of art therapy is used by trained art therapists to help individuals work though different thoughts, emotions, and struggles. You may be asking, why is the creative process important for those who are struggling. Well, there is a scientific reason for this. Our brain is split up into different parts. For the sake of explanation I will be focusing mainly on the logical brain (this is the prefrontal lobe) and the emotional brain (this is the Limbic system).

In the logical brain, this is where your brain remembers facts, statistics, language, and processes information (you guessed it) logically. In the emotional brain, this is where your brain stores memories of sound, touch, and smell. This part of the brain is emotional, intuitive, visual, spatial, and tactile. Brain scans show that when someone experiences trauma of some form, the prefrontal lobes become hypoactive and deactivate, while the limbic system becomes hyperactive. The traumatic memory is stored in the emotional brain and the experience becomes disconnected from the logical, prefrontal lobes. This is why when we experience hardships we often have a very difficult time verbalizing the experience, and words seem not to be enough, as our bodies remember the intensity and the emotions.

So how do we heal what we cannot speak?

Rather than relying solely on talking through our experiences, art can provide opportunities for us to express the emotions and sensations of our internal experience. This is why art is not just for those who are disturbed, it is for anyone that wants to connect with their internal experience and voice, and express their emotions and sensations through creativity. Art making can activate the prefrontal cortex by integrating both the emotional and rational brain. As a result, art can help individuals create meaning and understanding to their experiences and help the non-verbal become verbal.

With this in mind, this book aims to help individuals develop a therapeutic outlet of art making. This book does not provide art therapy in itself, but aims to be an additional resource for both clinicians and anyone that is looking for a self-care outlet. Connect with a licensed therapist if you are struggling and need additional help.

SETTING UP YOUR SACRED
SPACE FOR ART MAKING

In this book you will find therapeutic art activities. These activities are meant to provide space for you to turn inwards and to connect with your thoughts, feelings, and emotions.

To begin, I encourage you to engage with your art making as a sacred moment. Each activity will begin with a mindfulness exercise and intention. It is recommended to start with these mindful moments before art making so that you can get into the proper headspace and connect with your body, heart, mind, and emotions. After completing the meditation you may then follow the prompts to enter into art making. These art activities aim to help you connect with your emotions and tune inward as a form of self care.

And finally, it is encouraged that you spend some time reflecting over the experience once you are done creating. There will be a list of reflection questions after each art activity. You can slowly process through the questions to check in with how you are feeling. The activities should take roughly 30 minutes, but remain for however short or long you need. It may be likely that difficult emotions will come up as you engage in some of the therapeutic art activities. That is ok and natural.

Our emotions are not a bad thing, they are merely our bodies way of communicating to us. It is important to tune inwards and listen compassionately.

Before you start any of the activities in this book I recommend that you create a sacred space for your art making. Whether this is a physical space or not is your choice, but each time you arrive at the art practice you should set the stage to become fully present and focused. This is a time for you. Whatever makes you feel the most at home within your body and the most present- do this.

You can dedicate a corner of a quiet room for this practice, or set a specific time of the day or week to turn inwards and create. Do not be afraid to light a candle or some incense, turn off your phone, play soothing music, enjoy your favorite cup of tea, relish in the quiet moment, and pause. This is a time to let your inner voice sing without judgment. Enjoy the process. It is an emotional, physical, and spiritual journey of the self.

THERAPEUTIC ART
ACTIVITIES

PART I

THERAPEUTIC ART ACTIVITIES FOR JOY

Tell me the story, the one filled with joy
So that as you speak
Golden honey will pour from your voice
And you will see laughter as medicine
To life's poison of choice
And this joy you can't contain is a heavenly noise

Next, tell me the story, the one filled with pain
Where memories are lonely
Like being caught in the rain
But please don't you dare and forget as you share
That in the midst of December joy was found there
For the moments smell faintly of honey drenched air

— JOY IS MEDICINE, KA

1

ABUNDANCE

INTENTION:

To get started, get into a position you can comfortably hold. Once comfortable, gently close your eyes and begin to take deep, refreshing breaths. Allow each breath to ease your mind, and come into a still, focused state.

Inhale deeply.
And exhale it all out.

Turn inward and make yourself the first priority in this moment.

As you continue to breathe, focus on the journey of your breath throughout your body. Notice how it feels as it weaves throughout your muscles with each inhale, and how it relaxes you on each exhale. Allow your breath to ease any tightness you may be feeling.

Breathing in deeply.
And let it all go.

When any judgments come up, as they naturally will, acknowledge them and let them drift away.

Replace any negative thoughts of self criticism with loving ones, and thank your body for supporting you in this moment.

Inhale.
And exhale.

Next, open your eyes and tune into the present moment. Look around you at this sacred space.

What do you see?

What do you hear?

What do you smell?

Just breathe, and take in the fullness of this moment. Focus on your breathing, coming in and going out.

Breathe in deeply.
And let it all go.

Invite some intention before the art. Practice non-judgment and acceptance. There is no right or wrong way, just enjoy the process.

Repeat this with me out loud:

"Today, I give myself permission to create. I am clearing
my mind and opening my heart for creativity."

Breathing in deeply one last time.
And exhale, letting it all go.

Let's begin.

DIRECTIVE: GROWING ABUNDANCE TREE

1. Take a short walk outside to collect small branches, collect around 10. Make sure that they are around 6-12 inches long. This bundle of branches will be used as a foundation for your gratitude tree.
2. Next, take a small jar and fill the bottom of it with sand, stones, coins, or anything that you would like to keep inside, and add the branches to the jar as well. You can add meaningful items as well to the jar, such as letters, photographs, jewelry, etc.
3. Next, cut out leaves into patterned or colored paper and punch a hole in each of them.
4. Add what you are grateful for to each leaf.
5. Add string to the leaves so they can hang from the tree's branches.

SUPPLIES OF YOUR CHOICE:

- tree branches
- Jar
- Found objects to add to your jar: rocks, stones, glitter, buttons, coins, etc.
- Scrapbook paper/construction paper/card-stock/etc
- Pen
- Marker

PROCESS QUESTIONS:

1. What are you grateful for?
2. Did you face any resistance during this exercise?
3. Was there a point of celebration when creating this piece?
4. How are you feeling?
5. How was this experience?

HAPPINESS

INTENTION:

Let's take these next few moments to come back to our center, and to feel grounded and present.

Move into a comfortable, seated position. Gently close your eyes and shift your attention onto your breathing.

Inhale.
And exhale.

Feel it coming in and going out, your chest rising and falling. Take slower, deeper breaths than you normally would.

Breathing in deeply.
And letting it all go.

Take a deep breath in through your nose, and exhale slowly out through your mouth. Feel your lungs expand with each inhale, and contract with each exhale.

Inhale.
And exhale.

Next, connect with the sensations of your body. Tune into how it feels and notice if it is trying to tell you anything. Notice any tension that your body is holding. With each exhale soften anywhere you may be tightening. Relax.

Breathe in.
And let it all go.

Thank your body for how it carries you throughout the day, and how it holds you in this moment. Let it know that it has permission to relax.

If your mind starts to wander off, notice it, and bring your attention back to your body, using your breath as your guide.

Inhale deeply.
And exhale it all out.

Picture one thing that happened today that made you smile. Let that happy feeling fill you up, and breathe the feeling in through your nose.

Inhale.
And exhale.

Let yourself sit in the feeling of joy and happiness for a few minutes.

Breathing deeply.
And letting it all go.

Welcome yourself into this creative space. Treasure this

moment and acknowledge that you took time to tend to your heart today.

How is your heart?

Wrap your arms around yourself and give yourself a squeeze, you are loved.

Breathing in deeply.
And letting it go.

Invite some intention before the art. Practice non-judgment and acceptance. There is no right or wrong way, just enjoy the process.

Inhale.
Exhale.

And repeat this out loud with me:

"Today, I give myself permission to create. I am
clearing my mind and opening my heart for
creativity."

Breathe in deeply.
And let it all go.

Let's begin.

DIRECTIVE: A PERFECT DAY

1. draw your vision of a perfect day

2. visually depict your idea of a perfect day in whichever way you feel necessary with shapes, colors, and textures.

SUPPLIES OF YOUR CHOICE:

- White paper
- Pencils
- Pens
- Markers
- Oil pastels
- Colored pencils

PROCESS QUESTIONS:

1. What is your perfect day?
2. Are there any changes you can make to your daily life that will make it more enjoyable?
3. Did you face any resistance during this exercise?
4. Was there a point of celebration when creating this piece?
5. How are you feeling?
6. How was this experience?

GRATITUDE

INTENTION:

Get into a comfortable, seated position, and elongate your spine. Softly close your eyes. Focus your attention towards your body. Feel the ground beneath you, holding you.
Bring all of your awarenesses into your breath.

Breathing in deeply.
And letting it all go.

Notice how your breath flows in, and out. Allow your breath to flow all the way down, expanding into your stomach and ribcage.

Breathe in deeply.
And let it all go.

Hold at the top of your next inhale, and when you are ready release with a sigh.

Breathing deeply.
And letting it all go.

At the bottom of your last deep breath, return your breathing to a comfortable, normal effort, letting it flow naturally as if you didn't have to think about it.

Inhale.
And exhale.

As you breathe, take time to appreciate that your lungs are able to fill deeply and fully, to have fresh air flowing through your chest, and that you can have this moment to yourself. Give thanks for this very moment.

Inhale.
And exhale, let go.

Appreciate your heart and mind for keeping you alive.
Appreciate your body for holding you upright.
Appreciate your eyes for allowing you to see.
Appreciate your ears for allowing you to hear.
Appreciate your mouth for allowing you to taste.
Say out loud, "thank you".
There is so much that happens in our lives that is worthy for gratitude.
Tune in to the space surrounding you and give thinks. Give thanks that there is a planet with sunshine and beauty, and that it keeps us alive.
Let yourself be thankful for the mere fact that you exist.
There is beauty found in every moment if we take the time to look.

Inhale deeply.

And exhale it all out.

Wrap your arms around yourself and squeeze. Express gratitude towards yourself that you showed up as an act of self care. You are loved.

Inhaling deeply.
And exhale, let go.

Invite some intention before the art. There is no right or wrong way to create, practice non-judgment and acceptance. Just enjoy the process and let yourself create from your heart. Open your eyes and repeat with me:

"Today, I give myself permission to create. I am clearing
my mind and opening my heart for creativity."

Breathing in deeply one last time.
And letting it all go.

Let's begin.

DIRECTIVE:

1. Create art on sticky pads or note cards and write the words on each piece, "take time to be grateful today"
2. Keep these in places you will see throughout your day to remember to have moments of gratitude.

SUPPLIES OF YOUR CHOICE:

- Sticky notes
- Pen
- Crayons
- Markers
- Colored pencils

PROCESS QUESTIONS:

1. What are you grateful for today?
2. Where did you place your sticky notes?
3. Did you face any resistance during this exercise?
4. Was there a point of celebration when creating this piece?
5. How are you feeling?
6. How was this experience?

PLAY

INTENTION:

First, gently close your eyes. Begin by focusing on your breath, coming in and going out. Allow your breath to ground you into the present moment.

Inhale.
And exhale.

Give yourself the permission to focus on you.

There is nothing else you should be doing, and nowhere else you need to be outside of this present moment.

Breathe in deeply.
Let it all go.

Continue to take slow, mindful breaths, and allow each inhale to go deeper than the last.

Feel your chest rise and fall with each inhale and exhale.

Feel what you are sitting on and notice how it holds you.

Allow yourself to sink into the feeling of being held.

Inhale deeply.
And exhale, let it all go.

Notice if there is any tightness in the body. With your next exhale, relax anywhere you may be holding stress.

Relax your jaw, and let your shoulders drop down away from your ears.

Allow your breath to return to its normal rhythm, and breathe naturally.

Inhale.
And exhale.

Take time to just breathe.

Invite some intention before the art. Practice non-judgment and acceptance. There is no right or wrong way, just enjoy the process.

Repeat with me out loud:

"Today, I give myself permission to create. I am clearing
my mind and opening my heart for creativity."

Breathing in deeply one last time.
And exhale, let it all go.

Let's begin.

DIRECTIVE: PAINT TO MUSIC

1. Make a playlist of 3 songs that put you in a positive mood.
2. Put on headphones or play it through a speaker to paint to.
3. There is no right or wrong way to create, just let the music move you and create as you listen intuitively

SUPPLIES OF YOUR CHOICE:

- Device to play music through
- Headphones/ speaker
- Watercolor paper/ canvas/ Bristol board
- Watercolor paint
- Acrylic paint
- Cup with water
- Brushes
- Paper towel

PROCESS QUESTIONS:

1. What feelings does the word "play" evoke for you?
2. How can you add more play into your daily life?
3. Did you face any resistance during this exercise?
4. Was there a point of celebration when creating this piece?
5. How are you feeling?
6. How was this experience?

BEAUTY

INTENTION:

Take this opportunity to settle into a comfortable position. Enter into this grounding space and pause. Take a moment and thank yourself for showing up, for showing up for yourself, your mind, your wellbeing.

Check in with yourself. Check in with how you are feeling right now. Give yourself permission to let go into the present space.

Release any worries and anxieties from the day and focus on this present moment.

This creative space is a gift to yourself.

Close your eyes. Let any heaviness release.

We will begin by breathing. Place your hand over your heart and feel your chest move with your breath.

Inhale.
And exhale.

Breathe in deeply.
And let it all go.

Breathe in love.
Breathe in joy.
Breathe in compassion.
Breathe in peace.

Give yourself permission to be still. Imagine any heaviness in your spirit move down through your body, and out into the ground.
Inhale, and let your breath release through a long exhalation. As you breathe out, let go of all that is holding you back.

Breathing deeply.
And letting go.

As you breathe, notice what you smell. Notice the coming in and going out of your nose. Fill your lungs completely, and exhale.

Breathing in deeply.
And letting it all go.

Just breathe

Next, invite some intention before the art. Practice non-judgment and acceptance. There is no right or wrong way, just enjoy the process.

Repeat out loud with me:

*"Today, I give myself permission to create. I am clearing
my mind and opening my heart for creativity."*

*Breathing in deeply.
And letting it all go.*

Let's Begin.

DIRECTIVE: FROZEN IN TIME

1. Grab your camera and take photographs of things you find beautiful. Be intentional with what you are capturing.
2. You can choose to print the photos out and frame them, or make a scrapbook, or just have them digital.

SUPPLIES OF YOUR CHOICE:

- Camera
- Optional: printer, frames, items for scrapbook

PROCESS QUESTIONS:

1. What did you capture?
2. Is there anything you wanted to capture but couldn't?
3. Did you face any resistance during this exercise?
4. Was there a point of celebration when creating this piece?
5. How are you feeling?
6. How was this experience?

FREEDOM

INTENTION:

As we begin our practice today, take a moment to check in with yourself. Check in with your brain, your body, your heart. Check in with any tension you may be feeling, and as you notice areas of stress, exhale it out.

Begin to rest and settle in.

Breathe in.
Breathe it all out,

Thank yourself for taking this time to be still, to be present, and to become grounded with your breath.

Let go of any physical tension. Let your body relax.

Let your eyes be heavy, your jaw be loose, and let your shoulders draw towards the earth.

Breathe in,
And let it go.

Feel the stillness around you and take it all in.
Pause.
Stay with the awareness of your breath.
Notice it coming in and going out.

> *Breathing in deeply.*
> *And letting it all go*

Invite some intention before the art. Practice non-judgment and acceptance. There is no right or wrong way, just enjoy the process.

Read this with me out loud:

> *"Today, I give myself permission to create. I am clearing*
> *my mind and opening my heart for creativity."*

> *Breathing in deeply one last time.*
> *And exhale, letting it all go.*

Let's begin.

DIRECTIVE: FREEDOM

1. Think of a time that you felt free. What feelings come to mind? Do you still feel free today?
2. Create an image of what freedom means to you

SUPPLIES OF YOUR CHOICE:

- Paper/card-stock/Bristol board/ watercolor paper
- Markers
- Crayons
- Colored pencils
- Pens
- Acrylic paint
- Watercolor paint
- Pallet/ paper plate
- Paper towel

PROCESS QUESTIONS:

1. What feelings does the word "freedom" evoke for you?
2. Is there anything in your life hindering you from feeling free?
3. How can you feel more free in your own life today?
4. Did you face any resistance during this exercise?
5. Was there a point of celebration when creating this piece?
6. How are you feeling?
7. How was this experience?

PART II

THERAPEUTIC ART ACTIVITIES FOR LOSS

The trees now grow new life in each leaf
Yet this greenness is like a kind of grief
Because each new bud
Replaces golden memories
Of autumns where my heart would sing
In the crunch below feet wandering

Still there's beauty in these blooming trees
Where the birds return with buzzing bees
Yet I can't help but miss fall leaves
Where my feet would dance and my heart would sing
But I will let go and embrace the spring
And look forward to the new it brings.

— HELLO//GOODBYE, KA

7

LETTING GO

INTENTION:

Light some incense, or a candle, and grab a comforting drink.
Find a comfortable, seated position.
Close your eyes.
Feel your breath.

Breathe in deeply.
And exhale, let go.

Tune your heart and mind to the present moment.

This space is sacred.

Let's begin with 3, deep, centering breaths.

Inhale,
and exhale it all out.

Inhale deeply,

and exhale.

Inhale deeply,
and exhale, let it all go.

Allow yourself to come into this present state of awareness. You are here in this moment, connecting with all that you are.

Inhale,
and exhale.

The process of healing gives us the opportunity to realign ourselves. When life seems too difficult to handle, you are given this opportunity to rise. And here you are.

Breathe in,
and breathe out.

Let us take this opportunity to open our heart, and breathe deeply. Allow your breath to open your heart to love, peace, strength, and vitality.

Breathe in deeply,
breathe it out.

Feel your body.
Feel yourself grounded, supported, relaxed. Feel yourself held by the strength of the ground below you. Allow yourself to soften, to let go, and turn in.
Notice the breath coming in and going out.

Breathe in,
and breathe out.

Tune into your heart and notice any criticism, shame, sadness, or anger. What is it feeling?

Wrap your arms around yourself and squeeze. Release any guilt for showing up and taking time for yourself today. Instead, express gratitude for this moment.

Breathe in deeply,
and let it all go.

Invite some intention before the art. There is no right or wrong way to create, practice non-judgment and acceptance. Just enjoy the process and let yourself create from your heart.

Read this out loud with me:

"Today, I give myself permission to create. I am clearing
my mind and opening my heart for creativity."

Breathing in deeply one last time,
and exhale, let it all go.

Let's begin.

DIRECTIVE: A SWEET RELEASE

1. On a small piece of paper, write/ paint/ draw the things that are burdening you. Is there someone or something in your life that you need to let go of? Are there negative patterns, thoughts, and experiences that you would like to say goodbye to?
2. Fold the paper up and put it inside a deflated balloon/ attach it to the outside of the balloon with string.

3. Next, blow up the balloon.
4. Go on a walk and think about what you want to let go of and why.
5. Release the balloon when you are ready.

SUPPLIES OF YOUR CHOICE:

- Paper
- Pen
- Any decorating medium of choice
- Balloon
- Optional: hole punch and string to help you attach your art to the balloon if you choose to not put it inside

PROCESS QUESTIONS:

1. What did you place in the balloon and why?
2. Did you face any resistance during this exercise?
3. What was it like letting go of the balloon?
4. What is a point of celebration for you?
5. How are you feeling?
6. How was this experience for you?

8

REMEMBERING

INTENTION:

Welcome this moment with peace and softens.

Breathe deeply as you enter into a comfortable position.

Take a deep breath in and, as you let go, let yourself settle into the present awareness.

Breathe in deeply.
Exhale, letting go.

Let any heaviness exit out of your body with each exhalation.

Thank yourself for showing up, for committing to your self-care, and giving yourself this moment to just be.

Let any heaviness drop away from your body, and let it all go as you exhale.

Breathe in.
Let go.

Let go of any expectations of yourself, and simply embrace yourself exactly as you are in this moment. The only reality that truly matters is right now. You are exactly where you need to be.

Inhale deeply.
And exhale, release.

As you breathe tune into your heart. Remember that this is your story, and that you are creating each chapter every day. You are exactly where you need to be.

Breathe in deeply.
And let it all go.

Use the mantra "I am exactly where I need to be" whenever you feel your mind drifting away from the present moment. Focus on your breathing, coming in and going out.

Breathe in.
And out.

"I am exactly where I need to be."
Feel your chest rise and fall with each inhale and exhale. Feel what you are sitting on, notice how it holds you. Allow yourself to sink into the feeling of being held.

Breathe in deeply.
Breathe it out.

Invite some intention before the art. Practice non-judgment and acceptance. There is no right or wrong way, just enjoy the process.

·   ·   ·

Repeat with me out loud:

> *"Today, I give myself permission to create. I am clearing*
> *my mind and opening my heart for creativity."*

> *Breathe in deeply.*
> *And exhale, let it go.*

Let's begin.

DIRECTIVE: A PICTURE IS WORTH 1000 WORDS

1. Find photos of people/places/or things in your life that you miss.
2. Spend time reflecting on what it is you miss about these people/places/or things.
3. Create an art piece using these images.
4. You can collage them if you are comfortable, or create a memory box to keep them inside of.

SUPPLIES OF YOUR CHOICE:

- Meaningful photographs
- Optional: box
- Glue
- Brush
- Any additional supplies you would like to decorate your collage or memory box

PROCESS QUESTIONS:

1. What would you like to say to your collage/memory box? Are there photos of people or places that you would like to say something to?
2. What do you miss? Who do you miss?
3. Was there a point of celebration as you created your art?
4. How are you feeling?
5. How was this experience overall for you?

9

SAYING HELLO

INTENTION:

Let's begin today by finding a comfortable, seated position.
Close your eyes and rest your hands in your lap.
Take this time to settle into your body, into your being.
With your eyes closed, let any tension release out of your body, and down into the ground.

Inhale.
And exhale, let it all go.

As you enter into this space, pause. Release any worries and anxieties from the day and enter into this present moment.

This creative space is a gift to yourself.

Breathing deeply.
And letting go.

With your next inhalation, become aware of any sensations

in your body. Pay attention to the temperature and texture of air coming in through your nose as you take a breath in. Pay attention to the sensation of air leaving your nostrils as you breathe out. Notice the sound, the vibration in your body.

Allow yourself to find grounding, stillness, and peace within yourself.

Inhale.
Exhale.

Feel your chest move with your breath. As you breathe, notice what you smell. Notice the coming in and going out of your nose. Fill your lungs completely, and exhale.

Breathing deeply.
And letting it all go.

Tune out all external distractions, anything that might pull you away, and simply focus on connecting to your breath. Not thinking about your day, or what you have to do in the next 30 minutes, simply focus on the inhale, and exhale.

Breathe in deeply.
And exhale, let go.

Take time to remember that although we do not have control of what comes into our lives, we have the choice of how we respond. You are able to make choices from the center of your being: from love rather than fear, envy, anger, or shame.

Inhale.
And exhale.

Allow yourself to feel light. Feel any tension or negative

energy melt out of your body. With your inhalation, imagine yourself welcoming a radiant light into your body: a light of love, peace, passion, and joy.

Breathe in deeply.
And exhale, let it all go.

As we go deeper into this state of stillness, let us bring our attention to our breath, and our mind. Do not try to quiet your mind completely. As the thoughts come, let them come. Simply witness your thoughts without attachment. Stay present with your own breath, your own awareness.

Breathing in deeply.
And letting it all go.

Just breathe.

Invite some intention before the art. Practice non-judgment and acceptance. There is no right or wrong way, just enjoy the process.

Repeat out loud with me:

"Today, I give myself permission to create. I am clearing
my mind and opening my heart for creativity."

Breathing in deeply,
And exhale, letting it all go.

Let's Begin.

DIRECTIVE: BRING IN, LET GO

1. Look through magazines and find images of what you would like to bring into your life, and find what you would like to let go of.
2. Collage two different images: one of things to "bring in" to your life, and one of things to "let go" in your life.

SUPPLIES OF YOUR CHOICE:

- Magazines
- Glue
- Cardstock
- Brush
- Additional supplies of your choosing

PROCESS QUESTIONS:

1. What do you want to bring into your life?
2. What do you want to let go of?
3. Is there anything you want to change in your life after creating your art piece?
4. Check in with how you are feeling. How are you feeling?
5. How was this experience?

FINDING COMFORT IN TIMES OF GRIEF AND LOSS

ITENTION:

May we take the next 30 minutes to connect with our internal experience and the emotions that are within us.

Take a comfortable, seated position, rest your hands in your lap, and keep your elbows relaxed.

Close your eyes and take this opportunity to simply connect with your breath.

Inhale
And exhale.

Connect with the feeling of being alive. Feel a sense of gratitude for your heart beating, and your lungs breathing.

Inhale,
and exhale.

Breathe in love, breathe in joy, breathe in compassion.
With your exhale, open your heart to gratitude.

Thank you for being here.

Thank you for disconnecting to reconnect to your inner voice, and the love that is within you.

Breathe in deeply,
and let it go.

Give yourself permission to go deeper into this beautiful, meditative state.

Let go of what is to come today and simply give thanks for this moment.

Inhale,
and exhale.

Breathing in deeply.
And letting it all go.

May this day be a clean slate for your mind, for your being, for your actions, and for your thoughts.

Breathe in and welcome a feeling of renewal that is available within you, and around you.

Feel your breath in this moment. And say this centering thought in your head, "I am exactly where I need to be. I open myself to a higher power, to God, and trust the unfolding of my life."

Come back to your breath.

Inhale,
And exhale.

"I am exactly where I need to be. I open myself to a higher power, to God, and trust the unfolding of my life."

Take a deep breath in,
And let it go.

Feel your body, feel your love, your joy, your peace within you. Feel it filling you with positive, radiant light.

Breathing in deeply.
And exhale, letting it all go.

Invite some intention before the art. Practice non-judgment and acceptance. There is no right or wrong way, just enjoy the process.

Read this with me out loud:

"Today, I give myself permission to create. I am clearing
my mind and opening my heart for creativity."

Breathing in deeply one last time.
And exhale, let it all go.

Let's begin.

DIRECTIVE: COMFORT IN A BOX

1. Find a medium sized box
2. Think about things in your life that you find comforting or soothing
3. Put items into the box that fall under three categories: Personal strengths- Traits that you have that you are

proud of; Relational strengths- Aspects of
relationships that have felt loving or comforting to
you; Spiritual strengths- What nourishes your spirit.
This could be spiritual figures, nature, music, etc
4. Return to this box whenever you need to find a sense
comfort

SUPPLIES OF YOUR CHOICE:

- Box
- Some typical examples to include in a comfort box
  are: Encouraging notes from others, something soft
  to touch, putty, calming pictures, crystals, essential
  oils, etc.

PROCESS QUESTIONS:

1. What significant items did you add to your box?
2. Was there anything you added to your box that
   surprised you?
3. What feelings came up for you as you created
   this box?
4. Do you feel comforted? Or another feeling?
5. How was this experience overall?

NEW

INTENTION:

May we begin our journey today by reconnecting with ourselves. Closing the eyes, sitting comfortably, feeling the ground and surface underneath you.
Let's take a deep breath in, and let it all out.

Inhale.
And exhale.

Letting go of any heaviness that is weighing you down right now.

Inhale.
And exhale.

Give yourself permission to settle, to find stillness, and to find a connection with your heart.
Let go of any stress in your life, and allow yourself the permission to enjoy stillness in this moment.

Inhale peace, love, and the new that this season will bring.

Exhale any stress, anger, or sadness- letting go of the old.

Inhale and feel the coolness of the breath,

Exhale, and feel its warmth.

Let yourself be heavy, be gentle, be comforted by this moment of peace.

Breathe in,
breathe out.

Feel yourself grounded.

Let go and open yourself to the fullness of the present moment.

Focus on your breathing, coming in and going out.

Breathing in deeply.
And letting it all go.

How is your heart?

Acknowledge any feelings that you have come in with. Be encouraged that you are taking time out of your day to tend to your heart.

Inhale.
And exhale.

Invite some intention before the art. Practice non-judgment and acceptance. There is no right or wrong way, just enjoy the process.

Repeat out loud with me:

"Today, I give myself permission to create. I am clearing
my mind and opening my heart for creativity."

Let's begin.

DIRECTIVE: BRIDGE DRAWING

1. Draw a bridge. This can be a physical or metaphorical place.
2. Think of this bridge as your life's journey. On one end of the bridge create where you came from (or are at now), while on the other end, create the "new" that you want to find for your life.
3. Think about where you are currently at on the bridge. Are you in the beginning, middle, or end? Reflect on where you are at on the journey.

SUPPLIES OF YOUR CHOICE:

- Paper
- Pencils,
- Oil pastels,
- Collage,
- Crayons
- Markers

PROCESS QUESTIONS:

1. Where is the start of the bridge? What feelings come up for you about the beginning of the journey?

2. Where does the bridge end? How do you feel about the ending?
3. Where are you on the journey of your bridge?
4. How are you feeling?
5. How was this experience?

OLD

INTENTION:

Give yourself a moment to get into a comfortable, seated position.

Wherever you are, close your eyes and relax.

Tune into the inhalation, and the exhalation of your breath.

Breathing in deeply.
And letting it all go.

Thank yourself for showing up for your wellbeing and connection today. Focus on the very simple act of breathing in and out.

It's time to give yourself permission to find stillness and peace. To find a deeper connection within.

Breathe in,
and out.

Our choices either come from love or from fear. We always

have a choice to decide which voice to listen to, and to choose love over fear. The choice is yours, even if the situation isn't.

So breathe in deeply, and let yourself connect deeper with your heart.

Breathe in.
Breathe out.

Let yourself be still, calm, and present.

Breathe in.
And breathe it out.

Stay in the presence of your heart, welcoming a mantra to guide you through the process of focus, and stillness, "I choose love. Even when the world around me doesn't make sense, I choose love."

Tune into your heart. What is it feeling?

Breathe in deeply,
Breathe out and let go.

Shift your attention towards your body.

Feel the ground beneath you, holding you. Feel the breath coming in and going out.

Inhale.
And exhale.

Invite some intention before the art. There is no right or wrong way to create, practice non-judgment and acceptance. Just enjoy the process and let yourself create from your heart.

Read this out loud with me:

> *"Today, I give myself permission to create. I am clearing my mind and opening my heart for creativity."*
>
> *Breathing in deeply one last time.*
> *And exhale, letting it all go.*

Let's begin.

DIRECTIVE: MAKE A LIFE TIMELINE

1. Using a ruler, create a horizontal line
2. On one end of the line write the year you were born
3. On the other end write today
4. Fill in the memorable dates that come to mind. You can use symbols, words, and colors to help categorize them

SUPPLIES OF YOUR CHOICE:

- Ruler
- Pen/pencil
- Crayons
- Markers

PROCESS QUESTIONS:

1. How do you feel looking back over your life?
2. Are there any significant moments that stand out to you?
3. Are there any moments that you wish you could leave out of your timeline?
4. Are there any moments that you want to experience more of in the future?
5. How have certain events and experiences shaped who you are today?
6. How are you feeling?
7. How was this experience overall?

PART III

THERAPEUTIC ART ACTIVITIES FOR PEACE

I spend my time in forests, under the old, oak trees
And can feel the earth pulsing
With each mindful breath they breathe.
And as I look to the heavens,
Towards the wisdom laced leaves
I find a sweet solace here, in the silence and the breeze.
And I see long branches holding hands, in perfect unity
I'm reminded to rest, in the lessons of the trees.
While they inhale together and exhale in harmony
I'm breathing with them, and learning how to be.

— HERE, KA

13

RELAXATION

INTENTION:

Take a moment to get comfortable, finding a seated position, with your hands resting on your knees.

Close your eyes and simply focus on the sensations of your breath.

In and out.

Check in with how you are feeling in this moment.

Let go of tension.
Let go of heaviness.

Let go of any feelings that do not serve you in this present moment. Allow yourself to be.

Become aware of each inhalation, and exhalation.

Deep breath in.
And let it go.

Connect to your own stillness, to your own peaceful energy. Stay with your breath, go inward.

Inhale.
And exhale.

Take a deep breath in and look within. Look inside a little deeper, connect with your inner light. Let us speak this centering thought to help us melt into this stillness, "I am here, I am enough, I am worthy of love".

Breathe in.
Breathe out.

Tune in to the silence and let go.
"I am here, I am enough, I am worthy of love"
Breathe deeply.
Connect with your body. How does it feel? How is it to be in this space?
Focus on your breath, coming in and going out.

Breathe in deeply.
And let it all go.

Next, invite some intention before the art. Practice non-judgment and acceptance. There is no right or wrong way, just enjoy the process.
Repeat with me out loud:

"Today, I give myself permission to create. I am clearing
my mind and opening my heart for creativity."

Breathe in deeply one last time.
And let it all go.

Let's begin.

DIRECTIVE: CREATE A CALMING COLLAGE

1. Begin by entering into a space that is calming. Grab a soothing drink (such as tea), light a candle, grab a blanket
2. Next, choose images, colors, words, and whatever things that you find soothing, calming, or even meditative
3. combine these to create a collage to help you to relax.

SUPPLIES OF YOUR CHOICE:

- Mixed media: magazines, patterned paper, Washi Tape, stickers, feathers, buttons, etc.
- Glue
- Paint
- Palette
- Cup with water
- Brushes

PROCESS QUESTIONS:

1. What did you add to your collage?
2. Did you face any resistance during this exercise?
3. Was there a point of celebration when creating this piece?
4. How are you feeling?
5. How was this experience?

14

CENTERING

INTENTION:

We are going to gift ourselves a moment of stillness and peace, unplugging ourselves from a world of action and movement.

Give yourself this moment to go within.

Find a comfortable, seated position and have your palms open, resting comfortably on your knees.

Take a long inhale, feeling the oxygen enter into your body. And then slowly release everything with a gentle and calming exhalation.

Give yourself and your mind permission to settle into this moment.

Feel your body grounded, centered, and relaxed.

Breathe in.
And out.

You may be experiencing a lot of uncertainty in your life right now, but remember, with every challenge and pain you are faced with in life, incredible strength and courage can be developed within you to overcome.

Simply exhale, and let all of your fear and tension melt away out of your body, out of your mind, out of your being.

Inhale.
And exhale.

Remember that there is great power within you and you are able to do hard things.

Take a deep breath in and simply relax.

Everything is going to be ok.

Take another deep breath in, allowing yourself to settle down into the stillness in this moment.

Inhale.
And exhale.

Come back to yourself, connect with your heart. Release any tension that you are holding onto from the day. Feel the body slowly letting go. Feel the mind slowly letting go.

Be present in all that you are.

Breathe in.
And breathe out.

Welcome calmness and peace today by repeating a simple mantra of gratitude, "Thank you for breath. Thank you for strength. Thank you for life."

Find the smallest of gifts to be thankful for, and repeat them.

"Thank you for breath. Thank you for strength. Thank you for life."

Continue to repeat this and let your heart speak. Just send

your love and gratitude out through year heart, and see what comes up.

Let yourself be surrounded by this feeling of gratitude and love.

Breathe in.
And breathe out.

Invite some intention before the art. Practice non-judgment and acceptance. There is no right or wrong way, just enjoy the process.

Repeat with me out loud:

"Today, I give myself permission to create. I am clearing my mind and opening my heart for creativity."

Breathe in deeply.
And let it all go.

Let's begin.

DIRECTIVE: MINDFUL MANDALAS

1. Mandalas, meaning "circle", or "center" in Sanskrit, are circular and geometric patterns that are used to help individuals to focus and to enter into a meditative state. Today we are going to create our own mandalas to help us feel more centered.

2. Using a paper plate, begin from the outer edge and work your way inwards, adding circular and symmetrical patterns on the inside of the plate.
3. Allow the drawing to reveal itself and enter into a state of creative intuition and flow. Don't try and force anything or plan it out. Let yourself create anything you desire.
4. Notice how you feel before and after.

SUPPLIES OF YOUR CHOICE:

- Paper plate
- Markers
- Colored pencils
- Any other drawing supplies.

PROCESS QUESTIONS:

1. How will you incorporate mindful moments into your daily life?
2. Did you face any resistance during this exercise?
3. Was there a point of celebration when creating this piece?
4. How are you feeling?
5. How was this experience?

15

CONTENTMENT

INTENTION:

Taking this moment to find a comfortable place, become seated, grounded, and disconnected from all external noise. Let yourself go within.

Thank yourself for taking time out of your day to turn inward and tend to yourself.

Let us take this time to find peaceful presence.

Draw your awareness to your breath and close your eyes. Focus on each inhalation and exhalation.

Breathe in.
Breathe out.

Step into this moment knowing that you are worthy of a beautiful life, one that is founded on peace, gratitude, and love.

Feel your heart, the sensations of your breath, the coolness of the air coming into your body as you inhale, and the warm sensation of the breath leaving your body as you exhale. Allow this breath to ground you, to support you.

Inhale.
And exhale.

Ask yourself how you are doing. Look into your heart and feel.

Surrender to the moment. Release any tension you are holding in your body from the day. Whatever it is that is overwhelming you and causing stress, set aside for a moment and tune in to your surroundings, into the present moment.

Inhale.

And as you exhale, let go, into stillness. Surrender into stillness. As you go deeper into this beautiful silence, keep your present awareness on your breath.

Focus on your breath coming in and going out.

Inhale.
And exhale.

Invite some intention before the art. Practice non-judgment and acceptance. There is no right or wrong way, just enjoy the process.

Repeat with me out loud:

"Today, I give myself permission to create. I am clearing my mind and opening my heart for creativity."

Breathing in deeply,
And letting it all go.

Let's begin.

DIRECTIVE: FINDING CALM

1. Using a brush and watercolor paper, begin by wetting the paper with water.
2. Next, drip, brush, and splatter paint onto the wet paper.
3. As you do this, watch the colors merge and notice your feelings. Notice what you see when the different colors begin to make contact.
4. We are not working with particular shapes or forms for this exercise, we are letting go and allowing the paint to do all the work. When we let go of the need to impose form our minds can relax a little more.
5. Option: Use a straw to blow onto the surface of your wet paint, by doing this you will allow the paints to mix and blend together.
6. Suggestion: use only 2-3 colors for this painting

SUPPLIES OF YOUR CHOICE:

- Watercolor paper
- Paint
- Brushes
- Cup with water
- Optional: straw

PROCESS QUESTIONS:

1. When do you feel most calm or relaxed?

2. How do you keep yourself calm?
3. How are you feeling?
4. Are you feeling calm or another feeling?
5. How was this experience with the painting?

16

GROUNDING

INTENTION:

Welcome to this grounding meditation. Todays practice is going to be about finding stillness and remembering that no matter what happens throughout the day, there is strength within us that can help us get through any struggle we face.

With your spine straight and eyes closed, take a deep breath in.

Inhale.
And exhale.

Allow the exhalation to release any anxious, fearful energy that is holding you down in this moment. Allow the inhalation to give you a deeper connection with the peace in this moment.

Inhale.
And exhale.

Keeping your eyes closed and allow the body to let go of any physical tension. Relax your forehead, unclench your hands, allow your eyes to become heavier, relax your jaw, allow your shoulders to pull away from the ears.

Just inhale.
And exhale.

Let go of any thoughts, fears, and judgments that enter into your mind during this meditation. Witness your body letting go. Notice any sounds in the external world as you go deeper and deeper into this present state of awareness.

Inhale.
And exhale.

Notice your breath. Breathe deeply into the lungs. Allow more oxygen to enter into the body.

Inhale.
And exhale.

Notice the beat of your heart, the rhythm of life that is pulsing and vibrating through you.

Inhale.
And exhale.

Take a deep breath in and raise your arms above your head. Tilt your head up to the sky with your arms reaching upwards.

As you breathe out, bring your outstretched arms from the sky to your sides and bring your head to a neutral position. Move your body in whatever way you need to release tension and relax.

Bring your awareness back to your breathing, coming in and going out.

Inhale, feel your strength vibrating through your body. With this strength, know that you are able to overcome anything that challenges you in your human life.

Welcome this centering though into your mind, "Everything I need is within me. Everything I need is within me. Everything I need is within me."

Inhale.
And exhale.

Give yourself permission to feel, to heal, to breathe. "Everything I need is within me."

Inhale deeply.
And let it all go.

Invite some intention before the art. Practice non-judgment and acceptance. There is no right or wrong way, just enjoy the process.

Speak out loud with me:

"Today, I give myself permission to create. I am clearing
my mind and opening my heart for creativity."

Inhale deeply one last time.
And exhale, let it all go.

Let's begin.

DIRECTIVE: ROCK PAINTING

1. Paint rocks in whatever design you choose. Don't think about it too much and just allow yourself to enter into the creative flow. Focus on being grounded and steady as you create.
2. Go on a mindful walk and put your painted rocks out in nature.
3. Spend 10 minutes at the location that you drop the rocks off and practice being present and grounded. Take in the sights, smells, and sensations of the world around you, and connect with your body more than your mind.

SUPPLIES OF YOUR CHOICE:

- Rocks
- Acrylic paint
- Brush
- Cup of water
- Palette
- Paper towel

PROCESS QUESTIONS:

1. What did you paint on your rocks?
2. How did you feel as you were painting?
3. How did you feel as you spent time outside?
4. Did you face any resistance during this exercise?
5. Was there a point of celebration when creating this piece?

6. Do you feel more grounded after this exercise?
7. How was this experience?

17

FLOW

INTENTION:

Before we start, get comfortable. Remove any distractions and tune into your body.

Today we are going to connect to our inner voice within us, tune into our body, and connect with our inner self.

Settle into your position and, with a tall spine, rest your hands on your knees and gently close your eyes. Bring your awareness to your breath. Be aware of how the air feels moving through your nostrils, and out.

Inhale.
And exhale.

Do a quick scan of your body

Relax your face, relax your shoulders, slow and gently continue to breathe in, and out.

As your breathe out, let go of all that no longer serves you in this moment right now. Visualize all of the negative energy leave through your body.

Inhale.
And out.

Feel your heart in your chest. Let each beat in your heart radiate gratitude for this beautiful human life you have.

Breathe in.
And breathe out

Feel the sense of gratitude within you. Let this sense of gratitude fill you up.

Breathe in.
And breathe out.

Fell the air coming in and going out. Continue to breathe a couple of times here and give yourself a moment to settle down, to let go of any thoughts and worries, simply focusing on the breath you have and this moment you are given.

Breathe in.
And breathe it out.

As you release deeply into this moment, surrender.

Inhale deeply.
And exhale.

Invite some intention before the art. Practice non-judgment and acceptance. There is no right or wrong way, just enjoy the process.

Repeat out loud with me:

*"Today, I give myself permission to create. I am clearing
my mind and opening my heart for creativity."*

*Breathing in deeply.
And letting it all go.*

Let's begin.

DIRECTIVE: ZENTANGLE

1. Begin by creating simple, organic lines. Allow the lines to overlap in certain areas.
2. Then, fill in the different chunks of your design with a unique pattern. Each section should get a different pattern. Another option is to trace a circular object in different positions and have it overlap.
3. Fill all of the segments with patterns until the page is filled. You can also add color. The goal is to achieve a state of focus and flow.

SUPPLIES:

- Paper
- Black pens
- Colored pencils if desired.

PROCESS QUESTIONS:

1. Did you face any resistance during this exercise?

2. Was there a point of celebration when creating this piece?
3. How are you feeling?
4. How was this experience?

PART IV

THERAPEUTIC ART ACTIVITIES FOR ANXIETY

Even when I'm lost at sea,
and suffocated by anxiety,
As the water's grasp is drowning me,
I will still fight for land defiantly.

And I'll rage against this darkened storm,
And scream until my lungs are worn,
And I will cling to hope forevermore
As this will carry me safe to shore.

— HOPE IS AN ANCHOR, KA

18

FEAR

INTENTION:

As you come and settle into your comfortable position, take this opportunity to connect deeper to your breath.

Inhaling gently,
exhaling slowly.

Close your eyes and feel the sensation of stillness, easiness, and presence begin to overcome your body, guiding you to let go deeper and deeper into this moment.

Big breath in.
Big breath out.

Connect to your heart and thank yourself for finding this time out of your busy day, dedicating it to your health and wellbeing.

Give yourself permission to let go deeper. Feeling the heaviness of your body begin to melt into the ground. Allow yourself to be supported by the floor underneath you.

Breathe in.
And breathe out.

Go within.

As you allow yourself to go deeper, remind yourself that each day is gifted to you and you have the ability to mold it into whatever you wish. Just like a painter with a fresh, blank canvas in front of them, you have the power to create out of nothing. You hold the power to welcome each day with an inner strength, and to hold courage and understanding, releasing all fears and limiting beliefs of who you are. Let go of all self doubt and insecurity. A new day is here.

So breathe in,
And let it all go.

Choose now to step into courage. Breathe in and feel your breath entering into your body. Let it fill you up and guide you forward with strength. Stay with this awareness, this presence.

Breathing in.
And letting go.

Allow yourself to go deeper within. Use the following centering thought in this meditation, "With love and grace, I step forward with courage."

Breathe in
Let it go.

"With love and grace, I step forward with courage."

Observe any intrusive thoughts or fears. What are they saying to you? What do they feel like?

Breathe in.
Let it go.

Invite some intention before the art. Practice non-judgment and acceptance. There is no right or wrong way, just enjoy the process.

Read this out loud:

"Today, I give myself permission to create. I am clearing my mind and opening my heart for creativity."

Breathe it in.
And let it all go.

Let's begin.

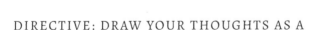

DIRECTIVE: DRAW YOUR THOUGHTS AS A CREATURE

1. Draw your fear/intrusive thoughts as a being or creature
2. Use whatever materials you feel necessary. Play around with shapes, colors, and textures.

SUPPLIES OF YOUR CHOICE:

- White paper,
- Pencils,
- Pens,
- Markers,
- Oil pastels,
- Magazines for collage
- Colored pencils.

PROCESS QUESTIONS:

1. What is making you most fearful? Are these things in or out of your control?
2. What are the things that are in your control?
3. Why does your creature look the way that it does?
4. Did you have any new insights after creating your art?
5. What helps you when you are feeling anxious?
6. What would you like to say to your Thought Creature?
7. Check in with how you are feeling. How are you feeling?
8. How was this experience overall?

19

NERVOUSNESS

INTENTION:

Our meditation today is going to focus on finding acceptance of all that we have in this life. When life throws things at us that are out of our control, we must surrender and let go instead of resisting the present moment.

You are alive, you are here. Worrying about what you cannot change, or things in the future will only cause you more stress.

With that, we will begin this mediation by getting into a comfortable position, closing our eyes, and bringing all of our awareness to our breath. Taking a deep breath into your nose, and slowly exhale all the air out.

Deep breath in,
And exhale all of it out.

One more deep breath in, and as you exhale, release all of your negative energy out of your body.

Deep breath in.

Exhale out.

Let go of any tension in your shoulders, and allow them to draw away from your ears.

Breathing in,
And taking a long, deep exhale out.

This is your time to be with yourself.

Deep breath in.
Exhale out.

Feel your heart, beating in your chest. Feel the rhythm of your heartbeat bringing you life.

Deep breath in,
And exhale out.

As you start to feel your body become more and more relaxed, slowly introduce our centering thought silently in your mind, "I surrender control, today is all I have. I surrender control, today is all I have. I surrender control, today is all I have."

Breathe in.
Exhale out.

Let go of anything that you have been holding onto from the day, and enter into the present moment.

Only this moment exists.

Tune into this sacred, creative space, becoming fully present here and now.

Breathing in deeply,
And letting it all go.

Invite some intention before your art making. Allow yourself to take the time to turn inward and to connect with your creativity. You deserve it.

As you create, practice non-judgment and acceptance. There is no right or wrong way to embark on the creative journey, just enjoy the process and let your heart sing.

Read this out loud:

"Today, I give myself permission to create. I am clearing
my mind and opening my heart for creativity."

Breathe in one last time,
And let it all go.

Let's begin.

DIRECTIVE: CONQUER YOUR FEARS

1. Create an image of something that scares you
2. Add yourself into the image conquering your fears

SUPPLIES OF YOUR CHOICE:

- Paper
- Medium of your choosing: paint, crayons, markers, colored pencils, etc.

PROCESS QUESTIONS:

1. What scares you?
2. How can you conquer your fears in your own life?
3. When was a time you were courageous?
4. How are you feeling?
5. How was this experience overall?

20

MINDFULNESS

INTENTION:

Welcome to this meditation practice. Todays intention is to find peace and mindfulness.

Begin in a comfortable position, close your eyes, and place both your hands over your heart. Take a deep breath in and listen to your own heart beating in your chest. With each beat, may you find the beauty in your life. With each beat, may it take you deeper within, into the internal experience.

Take a deep breath in and as you exhale, feel yourself become more grounded.

Slowly bring your hands down into your lap. Allow yourself to go deeper. Focus your awareness on your breath.

Breathe in,
And let it go.

Allow your body to let go of any tension in your face. Relax your forehead, allow your eyes to get heavy, and unclench your jaw. Bring this relaxation throughout your body, bringing your shoulders down towards the ground, relaxing your arms, your hands, your legs, and your feet.

Breathe in and notice the coolness of air entering through your nose.

As you breathe out, feel the warmth of breath leave your body,

It is very normal for our minds to want to cling to something. That is ok, simply remember to use your breath to come back to yourself in the present moment.

Take a deep breath in,
And a long, soft exhale out.

Breathe in.
Exhale out.

Breathe in and choose to let go of all of the negative energy you may be feeling. Choose to find peace in this current moment. Give yourself permission to feel, to be, to let go.

Breathe in.
Exhale out.

Notice your chest rise and fall with each breath and relax any tension in your body. Let go of all that no longer serves you.

Inhale.
Exhale.

Let's Invite some intention before the art. Practice non-judgment and acceptance. There is no right or wrong way, just enjoy the process.

Speak this out loud with me:

*"Today, I give myself permission to create. I am clearing
my mind and opening my heart for creativity."*

*Breathing in deeply,
And letting it all go.*

Let's begin.

DIRECTIVE: MEDITATION BEADS

1. Collect beads that appeal to you. They can be whatever you choose. Whether they are a similar shape, color, pattern, or completely different is up to you!

2. String the beads together (Fishing line or twine can work). If you would like to carry the meditation strand with you, choose beads that are small enough to fit in your pocket or bag.

3. Hold your meditation beads with one hand and touch one bead with the other hand.

4. With each bead you touch, complete one full breath cycle (inhale and exhale).

5. Move your fingers to the next bead, breathing in and out once per bead until you reach the end of your strand.

6. If you want to do another round, just move your fingers in the opposite direction until you reach the end of your chain, or until you feel a sense of calm

SUPPLIES OF YOUR CHOICE:

- Beads
- String of your choice

PROCESS QUESTIONS:

1. How will you incorporate mindful moments and these meditation beads into your own life?
2. How are you feeling?
3. Are you feeling mindful and present or another feeling?
4. How was this experience for you?

PART V

THERAPEUTIC ART ACTIVITIES FOR FAITH

And we must learn
From the moons gentle light
And dawn colored skies
To courageously arise
In dark places

— RESILIENCY, KA

21

POSSIBILITY

INTENTION:

Taking this moment, we will set an intention for our mindful practice today. Wherever you may be seated, close your eyes, and bring your awareness within.

Slowly breathing in, noticing every sensation of your breath as it enters your body.

Inhale.

And as you exhale, release not only the air, but any negative emotions and thoughts you have been feeling today.

Inhale.

Exhale into this beautiful stillness and presence.

Thank yourself for showing up today and taking time to tend to your wellbeing.

Inhale deeply.

And exhale slowly.

Connect deeper and deeper to your own heart. Connect with the space, with any emotions that are within you. And as you connect, remember that under all of the aches and pains within this world, love and peace can still be found. Even with doubt and fear in your mind, hope and courage can bloom in the darkest of places.

Breathing in,
And letting go.

Shift your attention towards your body. Feel the ground beneath you, holding you. Feel the breath coming in and going out.

Breathe in.
Let it all go.

Open yourself to the love that is here to guide your way forward in life.

As you go deeper into stillness, may love guide you as you release limitations and step into hope.

Breathe in.
Breathe out.

Repeat the following centering thought, "I allow myself to step into possibility, letting my inner strength and heart guide me. I allow myself to step into possibility, letting my inner strength and heart guide me."

Breathing in.
And letting it all go.

"I allow myself to step into possibility, letting my inner strength and heart guide me."

Breathe in.
Breathe out.

Invite some intention before the art. There is no right or wrong way to create, practice non-judgment and acceptance. Just enjoy the process and let yourself create from your heart.

Read this out loud with me:

"Today, I give myself permission to create. I am clearing my mind and opening my heart for creativity."

Breathe it in.
And let it all go.

Let's begin.

DIRECTIVE: SELF PORTRAIT

1. Fold your paper into thirds.
2. On each fold, create a past, present, and future self portrait.

SUPPLIES OF YOUR CHOICE:

- Paper
- Pencil

- Markers
- Colored pencils
- Crayons
- Oil pastel

PROCESS QUESTIONS:

1. What was it like creating the different parts of yourself?
2. Did anything surprise you about your self portraits?
3. Today, how can you step into what you hope for your future self to be?
4. Did you face any resistance during this exercise?
5. Was there a point of celebration when creating this piece?
6. How are you feeling?
7. How was this experience?

22

HOPE

INTENTION:

The focus on our meditative practice today is to find hope for the journey we are taking.

Achieving goals is only part of the journey, the process of becoming the best we can be is what truly makes the journey of life special.

When we find our self worth and inner strength, this helps us confidently continue the journey. Without the struggles, and without the hardships, the success and the victory will not taste as sweet. So as you move through your every day life, learn to accept whatever comes your way and focus on becoming the best you can be. Find gratitude so that you can open your heart and accept the life you have been given. Everything in your life is happening the way it needs to be. Trust the process and know that everything will be ok, and that beauty can be found even in the hardest of seasons.

With that said, find a comfortable seated position. Place your hands in your lap and close your eyes, deepening your breath.

Inhale and exhale, slowly and deeply.

With each exhale, allow yourself to let go of any negativity. With each exhale, allow yourself to go further into the present moment.

Tune into your heart. Let it remind you that you are alive and have felt deeply and fully.

Inhale.
And exhale.

Let go of anything that you have been holding onto from the day and enter into the present moment.

Only this moment exists.

Tune into this sacred, creative space, becoming fully present here and now.

Breathe in deeply.
And let it all go.

Let go of any thoughts or worries. Give yourself permission to tune into your breath. Gently let go.

Inhale.
And exhale out.

As you stay here with your breath, let's introduce our centering thought, "I surrender to the path of my own journey. I accept and embrace the process. "

Breathe in deeply,
And let it all go.

Invite some intention before your art making. Allow your-self to take the time to turn inward and to connect with your creativity. You deserve it.

As you create, practice non-judgment and acceptance. There is no right or wrong way to embark on the creative journey, just enjoy the process and let your heart sing.

Read this out loud:

> *"Today, I give myself permission to create. I am clearing my mind and opening my heart for creativity."*

> *Breathing in deeply one last time,*
> *And letting it all go.*

Let's begin.

DIRECTIVE: VISION

1. Think about what you hope for in life.
2. Create a vision board using words, phrases, and images.

SUPPLIES OF YOUR CHOICE:

- Cardboard/card-stock
- Magazines for collaging
- Stickers

- Markers
- Crayons

PROCESS QUESTIONS:

1. What feelings does the word "hope" evoke for you?
2. How are you going to achieve the things that you envision for your life?
3. Was there anything on your vision board that surprised you?
4. Was there anything on your vision board that discouraged you?
5. Did you face any resistance during this exercise?
6. Was there a point of celebration when creating this piece?
7. How are you feeling?
8. How was this experience?

23

COURAGE

INTENTION:

This guided meditation will focus on courage. Begin in a comfortable position and gently close your eyes.

Take 3, deep and empowering breaths. With every inhale feel refreshed. With every exhale release any fear from your mind.

Breathe in deeply,
And let it all go.

Tune into your breathing. Notice your chest rise and fall with each breath.

Breathing in, inhale.
And breathing out, exhale.

Is there any tension in your body?

Relax.

Breathe in deeply,
And let it all go.

What do you envision when you think of courage? As we think about our anxieties, our burdens and worries, summoning courage can feel like an overwhelming task, but courage does not mean that we are without fear. Courage is when we see the fear yet still believe that everything that we need is within our reach to overcome. That although the world brings about hardships, we can do hard things. Let us introduce our mantra, focusing on courage. Repeat with me, "This is hard, but I can do hard things. This is hard, but I can do hard things. This is hard, but I can do hard things."

Breathing in deeply,
And letting it all go.

"This is hard, but I can do hard things."

Breathing in courage,
And letting go of fear.

Breathe in deeply.
And let it all go.

Let's Invite some intention before the art. Practice non-judgment and acceptance. There is no right or wrong way, just enjoy the process.

Speak out loud with me:

"Today, I give myself permission to create. I am clearing
my mind and opening my heart for creativity."

Breathing in deeply,
And letting it all go

Let's begin.

DIRECTIVE: COURAGE IS NOT THE ABSENCE
OF FEAR

1. Document an experience when you did something
   you didn't think you could do
2. Think about what courage felt like in that moment.

SUPPLIES OF YOUR CHOICE:

- Card-stock/watercolor paper/ Bristol board
- Paint of your choice
- Cup with water
- Palette/ paper plate
- Paper towel

PROCESS QUESTIONS:

1. What feeling does the word "courage" evoke for you?
2. When was a time that you did something that you
   didn't think you could do?
3. What is something in your life that you want to do,
   but do not think you can?
4. How can you step into courage today?
5. Did you face any resistance during this exercise?

6. Was there a point of celebration when creating this piece?
7. How are you feeling?
8. How was this experience?

24

BRAVERY

INTENTION:

In todays meditation we are going to focus on letting go of all that no longer serves us. Any worries or stress that takes more than gives, we will consciously make a choice to let go. It takes strength to not let the negativity we face throughout our lives affect us. Let us instead focus on love, gratitude, and creativity.

In this moment right now, let's decide to let go of anything that may be bothering us. Make the decision to release any negativity like a rock we are releasing into the ocean. Watch it sink lower and lower until it is out of sight.

Let's use this moment to welcome love, positivity, and gratitude. Let's get comfortable and begin our meditation together.

Sitting in a comfortable position, start by closing your eyes, and bring all of your awareness to your breath. Take a deep breath in and a long exhale out.

Again, breathe in deeply.
Exhale, letting it all go.

Feel the ground underneath you. Allow yourself to completely let go and release.

Take another deep breath in,
And exhale out.

As you inhale, feel the coolness of air coming into your nose. As you exhale, become aware of the warmth of the air leaving your nose. Just bring all of your awareness to those sensations.

Inhale.
And exhale.

Bring your awareness to your face. Release any tension in your forehead, then slowly make your way towards your eyes, allowing them to feel heavy and keeping them closed. Relax your jaw, feeling your tongue resting gently in your mouth.

Inhale.
And exhale.

Bring your awareness to your heart. Feel the rhythm of it keeping you alive and healthy.

Deep breath into your nose,
And exhale out.

Bring the energy of gratitude into your heart. Give thanks for being alive. Allow that feeling of gratitude and happiness to fill your heart, and fill the rest of your body.

Inhale.
And exhale.

As you enter into this relaxed state, let's introduce our centering thought, "I am capable. I am brave. I can overcome."

Breathe in deeply
And let it all go.

Step into the creative space with a sense of curiosity, welcoming the possibilities before you.

As you are here, tune into your heart. How are you feeling today?

Breathe in deeply
And let it all go

Invite some intention before the art. Practice non-judgment and acceptance. There is no right or wrong way, just enjoy the process.

Repeat with me out loud:

"Today, I give myself permission to create. I am clearing
my mind and opening my heart for creativity."

Breathing in deeply one last time,
And letting it all go.

Let's begin.

DIRECTIVE: JAR OF STRENGTH

1. Think about what gets you through difficult times and write a list of coping strategies, enjoyable activities, things you love, empowering quotes, encouraging words, etc. Some coping strategies you can include are: exercising, taking a bath, meditating, asking for support, talking to a friend, establishing healthy boundaries, time management, positive self talk, yoga, going on a walk, etc.
2. Tear up different pieces of paper and write on each something from this list of things that give you strength.
3. Next, decorate a jar however you want.
4. Put all of the torn paper into the jar.
5. Place the jar somewhere you will see regularly.
6. The next time you are down, pull out one of the pieces from the jar and read it. If it is an activity complete it. If it is an encouraging word or quote take the words with you throughout the day.

SUPPLIES OF YOUR CHOICE:

- Jar
- Paper
- Pen
- Mixed medium of your choice to decorate the jar

PROCESS QUESTIONS:

1. What did you place in your jar?
2. How will you currently use this jar in your life?

3. Did you face any resistance during this exercise?
4. Was there a point of celebration when creating this piece?
5. How are you feeling?
6. How was this experience?

PART VI

THERAPEUTIC ART ACTIVITIES FOR ANGER

I am addicted to angrily brooding
The heartache in my past
One dose in the morning
And two right before bed

But maybe forgiveness
Is the elixir to ache
Instead of romancing
The bitter poison in my glass

— AA MEETING, KA

25

POWER

INTENTION:

Todays meditation is going to focus on inner strength and power. The focus is to find the powerful energy within you to help you overcome any struggles that the day may bring.

I believe each of us is stronger than we really think. Life is a beautiful journey that is not always easy, but we can find the strength and resiliency to overcome. Although you may have faced great trials and pain in your life, remember the ways that you have overcome. Don't let a difficult situation define you and make you believe that you are not strong enough to make it through. With that said, let's begin our mediation.

Coming to a comfortable sitting position, bring your hands to rest on your knees and keep your spine strong. Hold your palms open to symbolize an internal openness.

Close your eyes and bring all of your attention to your breath.

Inhale deeply into your nose.

Exhale slowly out. Allowing yourself to sink a little deeper into a relaxed, mediative state.

Inhale.
Exhale.

Deep breath in,
And a long exhale out.

Become aware of any sensations in your body.
Allow the feeling of relaxation to take over as you let go. Let go of any worries, anxieties, and to-do lists.

Take a deep breath in,
And a long exhale out.

Feel the coolness of air enter into your nose as you inhale, and the warmth of air as you breathe out.

Inhale.
And as you exhale, let go of all of your fear.

Inhale.
Exhale, let go of your insecurities.

Inhale, bring in strength.
Exhale.

Inhale, bring in power.
Exhale.

Inhale, breathe in confidence.
Exhale.

You are capable of creating a life you deserve, believe that for yourself. Any negative emotions that come up, let them go.
Let's introduce our centering thought for today. Repeat this

mantra throughout the mediation whenever you catch your mind wandering: "Strength surrounds me, love guides me, peace is here. Strength surrounds me, love guides me, peace is here."

Breathing in deeply,
And letting it all go.

"Strength surrounds me, love guides me, peace is here. Strength surrounds me, love guides me, peace is here."

Breathe in.
Let it go.

Invite some intention before the art. Practice non-judgment and acceptance. There is no right or wrong way, just enjoy the process.

Repeat with me out loud:

"Today, I give myself permission to create. I am clearing
my mind and opening my heart for creativity."

Breathing in deeply one last time,
And letting it all go.

Let's begin.

DIRECTIVE: DRAW YOURSELF AS A WARRIOR

1. Start thinking about yourself as a strong, capable person

2. Draw what you would look like as a warrior
3. What are the traits that you have? What weapons or armor are you wearing?
4. Is there something you would like to conquer?

SUPPLIES OF YOUR CHOICE:

- Paper
- Crayons
- Markers
- Colored Pencils
- Pen
- Pencil

PROCESS QUESTIONS:

1. Do you see yourself as a strong and capable person?
2. What were the traits you had as a warrior?
3. Is there something in your life that you would like to conquer?
4. How are you feeling?
5. How was this experience?

STRENGTH

INTENTION:

Today, this meditation is going to focus on finding balance, confidence, and strength within our body and being. Throughout our everyday life there may be situations that leave us feeling lost, unsettled, and deeply anxious. When we become overwhelmed we can feel restless and frustrated, we can struggle to ground ourselves, and find it difficult to still our bodies and mind.

We cannot control what life presents us with, but we can choose how we respond to whatever life may bring.

Let's begin our meditation.

Find a comfortable sitting position. Sit up tall and relaxed. Place your hands in your lap in a resting position. Let go of any tension in your shoulders and allow them to drop down, away from your ears. Close your eyes, feel the heaviness of your eyelids.

Take a deep breath in,
With your exhale, let go.

Let go of anything that bothered you today. Let go of anything that doesn't serve you in this moment. Let go and unclench your jaw. Feel your heart beating in your chest. Feel the chest rise and fall, as you gently breathe in and out. Let go.

As you surrender to this present moment, let's introduce our centering thought: "I am strong, I am grounded, I am rooted in my being. I am strong, I am grounded, I am rooted in my being. I am strong, I am grounded, I am rooted in my being."

Breathing in deeply.
Let it all go.

Tune into your body. How does it feel sitting in the position you are? Focus on your breath, coming in and going out.

Breathe in.
Let it go.

Next, invite some intention before the art. Practice non-judgment and acceptance. There is no right or wrong way, just enjoy the process.

Repeat with me out loud:

"Today, I give myself permission to create. I am clearing
my mind and opening my heart for creativity."

Breathe in deeply,
And let it all go.

Let's begin.

DIRECTIVE: STRENGTH

1. Think about something that makes you angry. Are you currently experiencing something that is really upsetting you? Tap into this anger. How does it feel? How can you turn this anger into strength?
2. Next, think about the word "strength". Has there been a time in your life that you have felt strong? Is there someone that you view as strong in your own life? What about them makes them strong?
3. Think about some of the problems in your own life that you need strength to overcome.
4. Next, create an art response to the word "strength". You can create a time in your life that you have felt strong, the feeling the word brings to you, how you hope to cultivate strength in your own life, etc.

SUPPLIES OF YOUR CHOICE:

- Paper
- Pen
- Pencil
- Colored Pencil
- Marker
- Crayon

PROCESS QUESTIONS:

1. What does strength mean to you?
2. When do you feel strong?

3. Are there any problems that you currently need strength to overcome? What can you do to overcome them?
4. Check in with how you are feeling. How are you feeling?
5. How was this experience?

27

FORGIVENESS

INTENTION:

Sit comfortably wherever you are. Take a deep breath in, and as you exhale close your eyes and let go. Let go into this internal awareness of peace, and love.

Inhale,
and exhale.

Thank yourself for showing up today, for making room in your day for peace, and well-being.

Our mindful practice today will be about letting go of any thoughts and emotions that no longer serve you and your greater potential.

Breathe in,
and release.

As you let go, repeat this centering thought to yourself, "I let go of all that no longer serves me. I let go of all that no longer serves me."

Breathe in,
and release.

Let yourself settle into this moment, your eyes heavy, face relaxed, letting your shoulders draw down, away from your ears. Feel yourself grounded and balanced.

Deep breath in,
and let it all go.

"I let go of all that no longer serves me."

As we prepare our heart and mind for art making, remember that everything you need for creativity is found within you.

Allow yourself to let go and be in the present moment.

It is a sacred space.

Inhale.
And exhale.

Roll your shoulders backwards and then forwards. Release any tension that you are holding onto from the day.

Breathe in deeply,
let it go.

Tune into your breath. Breathe in deeply and feel the air expand your chest. Breathe out through your mouth, creating a "shhhhhhh" noise, soothing yourself as you would a child.

Inhale.

And exhale.

Invite some intention before the art. Practice non-judgment and acceptance. There is no right or wrong way, just enjoy the process.

Repeat with me out loud:

> *"Today, I give myself permission to create. I am clearing my mind and opening my heart for creativity."*

> *Breathe in deeply one last time,*
> *And let it all go*

Let's begin.

DIRECTIVE: UNSENT POSTCARDS

1. Think about someone that you need to forgive in your life. What do you need to forgive them for? Is there something that you wish you could say to them but cannot? Have you told them how you are feeling?
2. Create a postcard you will never send to this person.
3. On one side of the paper, write your thoughts out to them about how they harmed you and how you are feeling. If you would like to forgive them, express this to them in the card and release the anger that you have towards them.
4. On the other side, create an art response to your writings.

SUPPLIES OF YOUR CHOICE:

- Cardstock
- Pencil
- Pen
- Paint
- Water
- Brushes
- Palette / paper plate
- Paper towel

PROCESS QUESTIONS:

1. Who did you make your postcard to?
2. What did you write to them?
3. Did you face any resistance during this exercise?
4. Were there any points of celebration for you when creating this piece?
5. Check in with how you are feeling. How are you feeling?
6. How was this experience for you?

28

FRUSTRATION

INTENTION:

In this moment, find a space to externally and internally disconnect from the outside noise. May we take this opportunity to let go of frustration. Simply fall into the sensation of peace in your heart. Find a comfortable, seated position. Rest your hands comfortably on your lap, close your eyes, and notice how you are feeling in this moment.

Inhale.
And exhale.

Take this opportunity to let go of any heaviness in your body and mind. Allow any tension to release out of your face. Relax your forehead, allow your eyes to become heavy, the jaw to be relaxed.

Inhale.
And exhale.

There is no more need to hold onto anger and frustration in this moment. Give yourself permission to rest, to find peace here and now.

Inhale.
And exhale.

Let go of your shoulders. Let them fall downward, away from your ears. Let go of any tension that the world may have brought to you today. Allow your arms to be heavy, soft, and relaxed. Feel your heart gently beating with each inhale and exhale, reminding you of this beautiful life that you have. Find gratitude in this moment.

Breathe in.
Let it go.

With every breath that you take, open your heart to gratitude, to love, to forgiveness. You are strong, you are beautiful, you are loved. Let this idea sit with you, as you slowly give yourself permission to relax. Let go of worries, uncertainty, frustration, and pain.

Breathing in deeply,
And letting it all go.

Inhale.
And exhale.

Notice your breath. Notice what comes to you as you begin to let go. Notice any images, colors, thoughts, or memories. Without any judgment, simply stay aware as you give yourself permission to relax deeper and deeper. Feel your body getting heavier as you let go. Breathe. Rest. Just let go.

Let yourself be filled with ease, peace, and deep loving relaxation.

Breathe in.
Breathe out.
And let go.

Invite some intention before the art. Practice non-judgment and acceptance. There is no right or wrong way, just enjoy the process.

Speak out loud with me:

"Today, I give myself permission to create. I am clearing
my mind and opening my heart for creativity."

Breathing in deeply,
And letting it all go

Let's begin.

DIRECTIVE: GET YOUR ANGER OUT

1. Make your own "clay".
2. Mix together: 1/2 cup salt, 1/2 cup water, 1 cup flour, food dye (any color, be creative!)
3. Acknowledge what you are angry about as you mix the ingredients together.
4. Release your tension by smashing, squeezing, and throwing the dough.

5. When you are ready to relax, fill the dough with essential oils that make you feel calm.
6. Breathe in and out deeply, and focus on the scent you are smelling.

SUPPLIES OF YOUR CHOICE:

- Salt
- Water
- Flour
- Food dye
- Newspaper to cover the surface you're working on
- Essential oils

PROCESS QUESTIONS:

1. What is something that came to mind that you are angry about?
2. How did it feel mixing, smashing, squeezing, and throwing your clay?
3. How was adding essential oils and focusing on your breath?
4. How are you feeling?
5. How was this experience?

PART VII

THERAPEUTIC ART ACTIVITIES FOR STRESS

Come sing me to sleep
With the lullaby that the earth sighs
While the heavens are kissed by starlight

My heart longs for rest
And to feel the tight breath in my chest
Exhale in peace

So I'll journey far away
Along earths latitude, and ocean blues
To find an oasis where I can breathe

— REST, KA

29

OVERWHELM

INTENTION:

Let us take a moment to let go of all of the anxiety and overwhelm that does not serve us.

We will begin by rolling out our shoulders, and releasing any tension that is stored in our body throughout the day. Begin to head roll to the right, and then to the left. Take some side body stretches, and then come back to center.

Rest your eyes, and place your hands on your knees.

Take a few deep breaths here. Bring all of your awareness to your breath.

Surrender to the moment.

Breathing in deeply,
And letting go.

Release any tension you are holding in your body from the day. Whatever it is that is overwhelming you and causing stress, set aside for a moment and tune in to your surroundings.

. . .

Focus on what you hear, smell, and touch.

Focus on your breathing, coming in and going out.

Breathe in deeply,
And let it all go.

As we are sitting here with our eyes closed, bring your mind to a happy place, it could be on the beach, or a cottage, or anywhere where you feel safe and happy. In your mind, allow yourself to fully let go of your body weight in your happy place. Take a deep breath in, gathering all of your energy that stressed you today. As you exhale, bring all of your energy, all of the things that weigh you down, out of your body.

Again, deep breath in,
And let it all go.

You are peaceful and safe here in this moment. You can take as many breaths as you like. Feel free to take some extra time to breathe and let go. And as you exhale, visualize yourself releasing what does not benefit you, and inhaling all positive energy into your body. Breathe in compassion, kindness and love. Breathe out negativity, anxiety, stress, and insecurities.

As you breathe in, inhale the present and what is to come. And as you exhale, let go of the old and release.

Breathe in deeply,
And let it all go.

Slowly, when you are ready, begin to gently move your fingers, becoming aware of your hands. As you open your eyes, feel yourself lighter, carefree, and content with where you are, and who you are.

Breathe in,
Let go.

Invite some intention before the art. Practice non-judgment and acceptance. There is no right or wrong way, just enjoy the process.

Repeat with me out loud:

"Today, I give myself permission to create. I am clearing
my mind and opening my heart for creativity."

Breathe in deeply,
And let it all go.

Let's begin.

DIRECTIVE: IN CONTROL OR OUT OF?

1. Make a list of things you can control right now
2. Create a large circle in the middle of the paper
3. Inside the circle, fill the space with what you control
4. While outside the circle, add things that you cannot control

SUPPLIES OF YOUR CHOICE:

- Markers
- Colored pencils
- Pastels
- Crayons
- Pencils
- Pens
- Watercolor paint
- Magazines to collage

PROCESS QUESTIONS:

1. What are things you can control?
2. What are things you cannot control?
3. How will you focus more on what you can control, and less on what you cannot?
4. How are you feeling?
5. How was this experience?

BURNOUT

INTENTION:

Start by sitting upright in a comfortable position. Inhale, reach the arms up to the sky. Exhale, bring the hands down to the heart.

Sit in an upright position and bring your hands to your knees. Begin to take a few, deep breaths to release any tension you may be feeling.

Deep breath in.
Exhale, let it all go.

Focus your intention on your breath. Feel the coolness as you breathe in through your nostrils, and the warmth as you exhale through your nostrils. Feel the present moment right now. Begin to deepen your breath, and release any tension on the exhale.

Step into this moment fully, abandoning self-criticism and allow yourself to be.

Breathing in deeply,
And letting it all go.

Check in with yourself emotionally. How are you doing today? How does your body feel?

Breathing in deeply,
And letting it all go.

Release any tension that you are holding, relax your shoulders down. If you are able, bring your head to one shoulder and then slowly bring it to the next. Roll your shoulders out, bringing them up towards your ears and then relaxing them down towards the ground.

Tilt your head up towards the sky, and then downwards. Moving as though you were saying, "yes". What will you say "yes" to in your life?

Look to the right past your shoulder, then look to the left past your shoulder. Moving your head back and forth slowly in a "no" movement. What will you say "no" to in your life?

Breathe in deeply,
And let it all go.

Invite some intention before the art. Practice non-judgment and acceptance. There is no right or wrong way, just enjoy the process.

Repeat out loud with me:

"Today, I give myself permission to create. I am clearing
my mind and opening my heart for creativity."

Breathing in deeply one last time,
And exhaling, letting it all go.

Let's begin.

DIRECTIVE: STRESS MONSTER

1. Visualize what is causing you stress
2. At the end of the visualization, think about what your stress would look like if it were a monster.
3. Depict this creature in a piece of art.

SUPPLIES OF YOUR CHOICE:

- Paper
- Markers
- Colored pencils
- Oil pastels
- Crayons
- Pens
- Pencils
- Magazines for collaging
- Modeling clay

PROCESS QUESTIONS:

1. What is causing you stress?
2. What steps can you take in the future to help you avoid burnout?

3. How are you feeling?
4. How was this experience overall?

FOCUS

INTENTION:

Taking the time to breathe, to connect with yourself, to calm your mind, and to ground is so beneficial to our spirits. With that said, find a comfortable position, close your eyes, and place your hands on your knees. Pay attention to the movement of your breath.
Take a deep breath in, feeling your chest expand, and as you exhale feel your chest contract.

Breathe in,
And exhale.

Bring your attention fully to your breath, letting go of any distractions, concerns, or negative thoughts.

Inhale.
And let it go, exhale.

It is normal to get distracted by thoughts, sounds, and restlessness, and to be pulled from the present moment. When this happens repeat to yourself the centering thought, "I am mindful in this present moment. I am mindful in this present moment. I am mindful in this present moment."

Release any worries and anxieties from the day and enter into this present moment.

This creative space is a gift to yourself.

Breathing in deeply,
And letting it all go.

Feel your chest move with your breath. As you breathe, notice what you smell. Notice the coming in and going out of your nose. Fill your lungs completely, and exhale.

Breathing in,
And letting go.

Next, invite some intention before the art. Practice non-judgment and acceptance. There is no right or wrong way, just enjoy the process.

Repeat out loud with me:

"Today, I give myself permission to create. I am clearing
my mind and opening my heart for creativity."

Breathing in deeply,
And letting it all go.

Let's Begin.

DIRECTIVE: CLUTTER COLLAGE

1. Create a clutter collage. Are there things cluttering up your life?
2. Use words and pictures to show the clutter in your life

SUPPLIES OF YOUR CHOICE:

- Card Stock
- Magazines for collaging
- Glue
- Brush
- Markers
- Colored pencils
- Pens
- Pencils
- Crayons
- Oil pastels

PROCESS QUESTIONS:

1. What are some of the things cluttering up your life?
2. How can you tangibly declutter these things and bring focus into your life?
3. How are you feeling?
4. How was this experience for you?

JUST BREATHE

INTENTION:

In todays meditation we are going to focus on being still and mindful of each breath, and in doing so, we are going to connect deeper with our inner self. By taking the time to slow down we are able to tune in and find peace.

Take a deep breath and find a comfortable, seated position. Find a place for yourself where it is peaceful and quiet.

Close your eyes and bring all of your awareness to your breath. Inhaling slowly and deeply through your nose, and exhaling deeply.

Allow your hands to rest on your knees. Feel the surface underneath your sit bones. Allow yourself to sink and melt into the ground. Let go. Allow your eyes to feel heavy, allow them to rest as you continue to breathe deeply. Let go. Simply allow your mind to take a pause from analyzing or thinking. Give yourself permission to rest.

Inhale.
And exhale.

Begin to feel your back elongated from the very base of your spine to the top of you head. Allow your shoulders to be relaxed and feel your belly rise and fall as you breathe through your nose.

Inhale.
And exhale.

Allow yourself to enjoy this present moment. Enjoy each inhalation and exhalation. If you notice any thoughts enter into your mind, do not become discouraged. Simply acknowledge that the thoughts are there and come back to your breath. Visualize your thoughts as clouds in the sky. Do not try and understand what they mean, just let them drift on by.

Inhale.
And exhale.

Let's introduce our centering thought of the day. Repeat this mantra with a confidence knowing that our words are powerful, "I am held by love, joy, and peace. I will hold on to hope even in the darkest moments."

Breathe in deeply,
And let it all go.

"I am held by love, joy, and peace. I will hold on to hope even in the darkest moments."
Focus on your breathing, coming in and going out. Focus on how the air feels moving through your nose and into your lungs.

Breathe in deeply,
And letting it all go.

Invite some intention before the art. Practice non-judgment and acceptance. There is no right or wrong way, just enjoy the process.

Repeat out loud with me:

"Today, I give myself permission to create. I am clearing my mind and opening my heart for creativity."

Breathing in deeply,
And letting it all go

Let's begin.

DIRECTIVE: PAINT WITH YOUR BREATH

1. Each time you breathe in, drag your paint brush upwards on your paper, all the way to the edge.
2. As you breathe out, drag your paint brush downwards, along the paper towards the opposite edge.
3. Repeat.
4. Do this exercise until the paper is completely filled with your brush strokes, until you cannot see any white paper left.

SUPPLIES:

- Watercolor paper
- Brush

- Watercolor paint
- Cup with water
- Paper Towel

PROCESS QUESTIONS:

1. When do you feel most calm or relaxed?
2. How do you keep yourself calm?
3. How are you feeling?
4. How was this experience with the painting?

PART VIII

THERAPEUTIC ART ACTIVITIES FOR SHAME

So I'll kiss my own fingertips
And I'll hug my gentle curves
And I will learn to show myself
The love that I deserve

And in the moonlight I'll be dancing
And romancing with the wind
With confidence and courage
I will find this love within

— A LOVE SONG, KA

SELF-ACCEPTANCE

INTENTION:

In todays meditation we will focus on self-acceptance. So often we focus on the future, constantly seeking more, instead of accepting everything as it is and accepting everything that we are.

Make yourself comfortable on a chair, on the floor, or on a cushion. Close your eyes and bring all of your attention to your breath.

Take a deep breath in,
And exhale out.

Deep breath in, and exhale, allowing yourself to sink deeper into your meditative state.

Breathe it in.
And let it go.

Surrender to the ground beneath you, and at the same time, feel your spine elongate towards the sky.

Breathe in,
And a long exhale out.

Take a moment to scan your body and notice any areas that, if possible, can be softened and released of tension. Become present with your breath, feeling the movement, feeling the temperature coming in and out of your body.

Inhale.
And slowly exhale.

With each breath, allow yourself to become more deeply relaxed. We will now introduce our centering thought for today, "I am doing enough. I have enough. I am enough. I am doing enough. I have enough. I am enough."

Breathing in deeply,
And letting it all go.

"I am doing enough. I have enough. I am enough."

Inhale.
Exhale it all out.

Invite some intention before the art. Practice non-judgment and acceptance. There is no right or wrong way, just enjoy the process.

Repeat with me out loud:

*"Today, I give myself permission to create. I am clearing
my mind and opening my heart for creativity."*

> *Breathing in deeply one last time,*
> *And letting it all go.*

Let's begin.

DIRECTIVE: "I AM COLLAGE"

1. Create an intuitive collage using "I am" statements.
2. Begin by writing on a sheet of paper statements about who you are.
3. Cut out the statements and collage them into a cohesive image on a separate sheet of paper.

SUPPLIES OF YOUR CHOICE:

- 2 sheets of paper
- Pen
- Markers
- Crayons
- Colored Pencils
- Glue

PROCESS QUESTIONS:

1. Which "I am" statement resonated most with you?
2. Did you face any resistance during this exercise?

3. Was there a point of celebration when creating this piece?
4. How are you feeling?
5. How was this experience?

SELF-LOVE

INTENTION:

Todays meditation will focus on peace, centering, and self-love. Thank yourself for taking time to tune inwards and tend to yourself.

Come into a seated position, with your back straight and eyes closed.

Take a deep breath in,
And exhale out.

Exhale out any feelings of insecurities, self criticism, frustration, and fear.

Inhale.
And exhale.

Inhale deeply into your own heart. Feel the strength of your heart, feel the beauty of your heart, feel the power of your heart, feel the love of your heart.

Inhale.

And as you exhale, let go of any negative thoughts that you don't have room for anymore. Empty it all out. Let go of the fear, of the shame, of the doubt. You are powerful, loved, whole, enough. Let it go.

Inhale.
And exhale.

Stay with your breath. Notice any sensations that begin to arise within your body and your mind. Don't attach yourself to anything but the inhalation and exhalation. Let each breath guide your heart to gratitude and love. Find gratitude for this day, for your strong and healthy body, and for your creative and powerful mind.

Inhale.
And exhale.

Stay here for a moment. Simply being aware of your breath and presence. Thank you for being here. Never forget that you are powerful, that you are strong, and that you are loved.

As you breathe deeply, notice where your breath flows into your body. Notice how it feels and what sensations arise with each breath.

Breathing in deeply,
And letting it all go.

There is no need to control the breath, simply use the awareness of your breath to discover what you are feeling, and to bring mindfulness to this process. Each breath is your opportunity to be fully present. Use your breath as an anchor to ground you in this moment.

Accept yourself exactly as you are.

You are enough.

Breathing in deeply,
And letting it all go.

Invite some intention before the art. Practice non-judgment and acceptance. There is no right or wrong way, just enjoy the process.

Repeat with me out loud:

"Today, I give myself permission to create. I am clearing
my mind and opening my heart for creativity."

Breathe in deeply one last time,
And let it all go.

Let's begin.

DIRECTIVE: POSITIVE TRAITS

1. Create a list the qualities that you appreciate most about yourself.
2. Next, create art about each positive trait.

SUPPLIES:

- Paper
- Pen
- Pencil
- Colored pencil
- Crayon
- Markers

PROCESS QUESTIONS:

1. How is your self esteem after creating this piece?
2. Do you struggle to see your positive traits?
3. What positive traits do you wish to develop more?
4. Did you face any resistance during this exercise?
5. Was there a point of celebration when creating this piece?
6. How are you feeling?
7. How was this experience for you?

35

SELF-COMPASSION

INTENTION:

We live in a busy, over-scheduled world, where we often feel the need to do it all and to do it perfectly. This can cause us to get stuck in insecurity. Today we will introduce compassion with our life as it is, and to find peace and grace from within.

Make yourself comfortable and remove all distractions.

Gently close your eyes and take a deep breath in, deeper than any breath you've taken today. Allow your breath to ground yourself in this moment. Give yourself permission to focus on you, there is nowhere else you need to be. There is nothing else you need to be doing except taking time for self-care.

Notice how your breath flows in through your nose. Notice how it fills you up. Encourage each natural out breath to release any tension. Observe every breath and allow it to deepen naturally.

Breathe in.
Let it go.

Give yourself permission to be fully supported by the ground below you. Slowly begin to scan your body and find ease. Relax your feet. Release your lower legs and knees. Feel your body become heavy as you let go. Find a sense of ease in your thighs and hips. Take a deep breath and release any tightness in your back. Welcome a softening into your abdomen. Let your chest and arms rest heavy. Feel your neck and shoulders release any physical tension. Allow your jaw to unclench and your cheeks, eyes, and forehead to soften. Let go.

Breathe in deeply,
And let it all go.

Become aware of any thoughts and emotions that come up without judgment. We will now bring in our centering thought of this meditation. You can come back to this mantra if your mind begins to wander. Repeat softly in your mind, "I am enough, just as I am. I do not need to be perfect, I am doing the best that I can. I am enough, just as I am. I do not need to be perfect, I am doing the best that I can."

Breathe in deeply,
And let it all go.

"I am enough, just as I am. I do not need to be perfect, I am doing the best that I can."

Breathing in,
And letting it all go.

Invite some intention before the art. Practice non-judgment and acceptance. There is no right or wrong way, just enjoy the process.

Repeat with me out loud: "

> *Today, I give myself permission to create. I am clearing*
> *my mind and opening my heart for creativity."*

> > *Breathe in deeply one last time,*
> > *And let it all go.*

Let's begin.

DIRECTIVE: DRAW YOURSELF AS A TREE

1. In the roots of the tree, write what gives you strength and your good qualities.
2. In the leaves, write the things that you're trying to change.

SUPPLIES:

- Paper
- Pen
- Pencil
- Crayons
- Markers
- Colored pencils

PROCESS QUESTIONS:

1. What did you write in the roots?
2. What did you write in the leaves?
3. How will you improve the parts of you that you would like to change?
4. Did you face any resistance during this exercise?
5. Was there a point of celebration when creating this piece?
6. How are you feeling?
7. How was this experience?

36

SELF-FORGIVENESS

INTENTION:

Todays meditation will focus on forgiveness. We will be focusing on letting go of anything that is weighing us down. It can be very hard to let go of past experiences and our past mistakes. This energy of shame that we are holding on to can hinder us from living from a place of confidence, love, and happiness.

We will begin by taking a moment to be grounded.

Get into a comfortable position, and rest your hands on your knees. Close your eyes, and bring your awareness to your breath. Begin to take slow, deep breaths. Allow each inhale to ease your mind and body, and bring you into the present moment. This is a time for yourself. Notice your breath coming in and going out, and the feeling of being grounded. Allow your breath to relax you.

Deep breath in.
And let it go.

Allow each breath to take you into a more relaxed state of being. Relax your forehead, allow your eyes to feel heavy and unclench your jaw. Let go of any tension in your face and allow this relaxation to travel into your shoulders, down through your back, and into the ground.

Inhale,
And let it go.

Big breath in.
And exhale.

Pay attention to the sensations in your body as you inhale. And as you exhale, see if you can become a little more relaxed.

Inhale.
And exhale.

Take notice of your thoughts and any distractions. Take a deeper breath in, and allow any negativity to be released from your body as you exhale.

Continue to breathe. Allowing your mind to settle and focus on the inhalation and exhalation.

Let's now take this time to introduce our centering thought. Repeating this mantra throughout this meditation, "I am still learning. I am human. I am still learning. I am human."

This is your time to let go of that which keeps you from moving forward in your life.

"I am still learning. I am human."

Breathing in deeply,
And letting it all go.

Settle into an intention as you create today. Practice non-judgment and acceptance. There is no right or wrong way, just enjoy the process.

As we focus on self forgiveness today, say out loud with me:

> *"I forgive myself for making the same mistakes more than once. I forgive myself for thinking that my energy and time were not valuable. I forgive myself so that I can move forward.*
>
> *Today, I give myself permission to create. I am clearing my mind and opening my heart for creativity."*
>
> *Breathe in deeply,*
> *And let it all go.*

Let's begin.

DIRECTIVE: PLANT SEEDS OF FORGIVENESS

1. Think of the areas that you need to forgive yourself.
2. On the inside of a pot, paint an image representing the things that are weighing you down/the ways you are holding onto un-forgiveness towards yourself.
3. On the outside of the pot, paint images and words of grace and compassion. The pot represents your heart.
4. Fill the pot with soil until you cannot see the inside image anymore and plant flower seeds.
5. Keep the pot in a place you will look at daily. The pot is there to remind you that even though you are not perfect, beauty can still be found despite our mistakes.

6. Each time you water it, remind yourself to be compassionate towards yourself as well.

SUPPLIES:

- Terra Cotta flower pot (or a disposable plastic cup will work)
- Acrylic paint
- Brush
- Paper
- Pallet / paper plate
- Soil
- Seeds
- Water

PROCESS QUESTIONS:

1. What do you need to forgive yourself for?
2. How you can be more gentle and compassionate towards yourself the next time you make a mistake?
3. Did you face any resistance during this exercise?
4. Was there a point of celebration when creating this piece?
5. Check in with how you are feeling. How are you feeling?
6. How was this experience?

37

SELF-CONFIDENCE

INTENTION:

As we move through our lives, doubts and insecurities can overwhelm us. In our most vulnerable moments, whispers of insecurities and mistakes define us.

Today we are focusing on self-confidence.

Take a deep, steadying breath and know that you are loved.

Begin by finding a comfortable seat, any seat that feels comfortable and puts you at ease is fine.

Once you find a grounding position focus on your breathing. Tune into the sensations of your natural breath rhythm. Breathe into the diaphragm. This will send sensations to your mind to relax.

Breathing in deeply,
And letting it all go.

As you breathe in repeat,

"rising, rising, rising"

And as you breathe out repeat,

"falling, falling, falling"

Breathe in deeply,
"rising, rising, rising."
Let it all go,
"falling, falling, falling."

As we see lack and insignificance in ourselves, remember that your life matters, you are valuable, and you are loved. Let's introduce our mantra for this meditation, "I matter. I am valuable. I am capable. I am loved."

Breathe in deeply,
And exhale it all out.

"I matter. I am valuable. I am capable. I am loved."

Breathe in.
Let it go.

We will invite some intention before the art. Practice non-judgment and acceptance. There is no right or wrong way, just enjoy the process.

Repeat out loud with me,

*"Today, I give myself permission to create. I am clearing
my mind and opening my heart for creativity."*

*Breathe in deeply,
And let it all go.*

Let's begin.

DIRECTIVE: MY LIFE AS AN ALBUM

1. If your life was an album, what would the title and art be?
2. Create album art symbolizing who you are, and your favorite things about your life.
3. On the back of the album art, think through a list of ten "songs" i.e. 10 traits or accomplishments that you are proud of and write them down.
4. Listen to music while you create that makes you feel confident.

SUPPLIES OF YOUR CHOICE:

- Card stock
- Acrylic paint
- Brushes
- Cup with water
- Pens
- Pencils
- Markers
- Colored pencils
- Oil Pastels

PROCESS QUESTIONS:

1. What did you title your album?
2. What traits and accomplishments did you think of while you were creating this piece?
3. What music did you listen to?
4. Did you face any resistance during this exercise?
5. Was there a point of celebration when creating this piece?
6. How are you feeling?
7. How was this experience?

PART IX

THERAPEUTIC ART ACTIVITIES FOR SAFETY

If a home could talk the walls would seep with ink,
As it writes the sweet memories
That stain the carpet and fill the kitchen sink.
The aroma of honey lingers
In the story the home speaks,
Of tender words each morning,
Filled with coffee and hot drinks.
The floorboards, painted yellow
From the heavenly sunrise,
Gently creek with softened feet,
As the birds come alive.
Here pain and laughter echo
In passing days of each week,
As it becomes the balm, a place of rest that many seek.
And the home would delight in the safety that it brings,
Sharing the secrets that it tells
In the walls that seep with ink.

— HOME, KA

EMBODIMENT

INTENTION:

Let's begin our mediation today by finding a comfortable position. Place your hands on your knees with your palms facing upwards. Close your eyes and simply begin to witness your breath. Feel the inhale of the breath coming in through your nostrils, and exhale out.

Inhale in,
And long exhale out.

Let go of all tension in your body. Begin to feel the movement of your breath in your body without trying to control it. Completely surrender yourself to your breath.

Deep inhale into your nose.
Long exhale out through your nose.

Feel your body slightly expand as you inhale. As you exhale, notice your chest contract and belly lowering. Allow the mind and body to become still and bring your awareness fully to the breath. Take a deep breath in through your diaphragm, and breathe out through your nose.

Inhale.
And exhale.

Take a deep breath in and fill your lungs with as much oxygen as you can. Exhale completely.

If you become distracted by a sensation, sound, or thought, gently bring your attention back to your breathing. Focus on the inhale and exhale. Be patient with yourself and with your mind. Through meditation we learn to have patience with our mind, and patience with our bodies. And this same patience will develop in our every day lives. Stay with your breath.

Inhale in.
And exhale out.

Take one more deep breath before allowing it to flow naturally on its own. As you breathe, imagine yourself breathing in compassion and love, and breathing out your fears, sadness, anger, and pain.

Breathe in deeply.
And let it all go.

Invite some intention before the art. Practice non-judgment and acceptance. There is no right or wrong way, just enjoy the process.

Repeat with me out loud:

*"Today, I give myself permission to create. I am clearing
my mind and opening my heart for creativity."*

*Breathing in deeply,
And let it all go.*

Let's begin.

Directive: Tune In

1. Draw a simple outline of your body on a sheet of
   paper.
2. Using color, lines, and shapes, fill in the areas of your
   body where you feel tension, stress, emotions, or pain.
3. Focus in on each spot and write down what
   sensations are happening in your body, both good and
   bad, and what may be causing it.
4. Journal about the experience and process what would
   make you feel better.

SUPPLIES OF YOUR CHOICE:

- Card Stock
- Marker
- Colored pencils
- Crayons
- Oil Pastels

PROCESS QUESTIONS:

1. Where in your body did you notice any tension, emotion, stress, or pain?
2. What is causing this tension, emotion, stress, or pain?
3. How can you find a sense of ease?
4. Did you face any resistance during this exercise?
5. Was there a point of celebration when creating this piece?
6. How are you feeling?
7. How was this experience?

HOME

INTENTION:

Sit in a posture that is relaxed and comfortable. Close your eyes and let your awareness go inwards. Welcome this moment of calm and release any pressure or expectations to be anywhere else, or to be doing anything else. This moment is a gift to yourself. Welcome home to your body.

Next, focus on your breathing. Follow your breath as it comes in and out. Breath by breath. Moment by moment.

Take a deep breath in,
And a long exhale out.

Inhale.
Exhale, let it go.

Inhale into your belly, feeling it expand outward.
Exhale, letting it all go.

Inhale, feeling your ribs expand outward into space,

Exhale, letting all of the air leave from your body.

Tune into your body. Notice how it is feeling. Allow any tension in your body to become released.

Breathing in deeply,
And letting it all go.

We will introduce our centering thought for this meditation, "My body is my home. It is mine, I am safe, I am home. My body is my home. It is mine, I am safe, I am home."

Breathing in deeply,
And let it all go.

"My body is my home. It is mine, I am safe, I am home."

Breathe in deeply,
And let it all go.

Invite some intention before the art. Practice non-judgment and acceptance. You are enough as you are. You are loved. You are healing. You are doing the best you can. Let go of any expectations with today's practice. There is no right or wrong way, just enjoy the process.

Repeat with me out loud:

"Today, I give myself permission to create. I am clearing
my mind and opening my heart for creativity."

Breathing in deeply,
And letting it all go.

Let's begin.

DIRECTIVE: SAFE SPACE

1. create an image of a safe, warm place that feels like home to you.

SUPPLIES OF YOUR CHOICE:

- Paper
- Oil pastel
- Chalk pastel
- Markers
- Crayons
- Colored pencil

PROCESS QUESTIONS:

1. What feelings does the word "home" evoke for you?
2. Where is your safe space?
3. Did you face any resistance during this exercise?
4. Was there a point of celebration when creating this piece?
5. How are you feeling?
6. How was this experience?

WHOLENESS

INTENTION:

Take a moment to settle into a comfortable, seated position, with your spine upright and your eyes closed. Begin to focus on your breath.

Inhale.
And exhale.

Find stillness, peace, wholeness, and grounding, as you give yourself permission to pause.

Inhale.
And a long exhale out.

Thank yourself for showing up today for your wellbeing.

Give yourself the opportunity to fully let go. Let go of tension in your face. Relax your jaw, your shoulders, allow your heart to be open. Allow yourself to be still. Surrender. There is a peace that grows within us when we let go and surrender to the process of life. Peace comes when we embrace the fluid journey, and release control. Let go. It's going to be ok.

Breathe deeply, breathe it in.
And breathe out, let go.

Open yourself to the flow of life. Let go.

Breathe it all in.
And let it all go.

When we surrender, we let go of the resistance, and open ourselves to trust our hearts, our intuition, God, the divine. With each breath you breathe, trust the unfolding of your life.

Breathe in,
And let it go.

Feel yourself grounded and release into the stillness, into peace, into wholeness, into love. As you go deeper within, let us introduce our thought today. You can go back to this mantra whenever your mind drifts. Repeat quietly in your thoughts, "I surrender to the flow and unfolding of my life. I trust my heart, my intuition, and the divine to guide me."

Breathe in deeply,
Let it all go.

Focus on the inhale and exhale of your breathing. Breathe deeply and give your body permission to be still and relax.

"I surrender to the flow and unfolding of my life. I trust my heart, my intuition, and the divine to guide me."

Breathe in.

Let it go.

Invite some intention before the art. Practice non-judgment and acceptance. There is no right or wrong way, just enjoy the process.

> *Breathe in deeply,*
> *And let it all go.*

Repeat with me out loud:

> *"Today, I give myself permission to create. I am clearing my mind and opening my heart for creativity."*

> *Breathing in deeply one last time,*
> *And letting it all go.*

Let's begin.

DIRECTIVE: AFFIRMATION ART

1. Find an encouraging statement that resonates with you. It can be a mantra, quote, scripture, desires for yourself, etc.
2. Write the encouraging statement on a sheet of paper and create art on the paper around it.

SUPPLIES OF YOUR CHOOSING:

- Card-stock/watercolor paper
- Pen
- Markers
- Watercolor paint
- Acrylic paint
- Glue
- Magazines
- Anything of your choice!

PROCESS QUESTIONS:

1. What encouraging statement did you choose and why?
2. Did you face any resistance during this exercise?
3. Was there a point of celebration when creating this piece?
4. Check in with how you are feeling. How are you feeling after creating?
5. How was this experience?

41

CONNECTION

INTENTION:

Todays meditation is going to focus on finding peace and connection with this moment. Often we get overwhelmed by the past or the future and we lose sight of the present moment. When we let go of the past and accept where we are right now we can find peace in the current moment. Being present frees us from the burden of tomorrow, and helps us to focus on creating a better version of ourselves today.

Let's begin our mediation. Get into a comfortable, seated position and rest your hands on your knees.

Take a deep breath in.
And let it all go.

Release any tension.

Inhale.
And exhale.

Let yourself release into the breath.

Inhale.
Exhale.

Settle into a comfortable position of ease. Imagine a string at the top of your head that is holding you nice and tall. Allow your shoulders to become fully relaxed and breathe deeply into your diaphragm. Tune into the sensations of your body. Listen compassionately to your heart.

Pause.

Focus on your breathing and follow each breath intentionally. Notice each inhalation and exhalation. Notice how it feels going in and out of your lungs. Allow yourself to become more and more relaxed, and at ease.

Deep breath into your nose,
And exhale, let it go.

We will introduce our centering thought for the day. Staying in a nice, comfortable, and relaxed position, repeat this in your mind: "I am exactly where I need to be. I am exactly where I need to be. I am exactly where I need to be."

Breathing in deeply,
And let it all go.

"I am exactly where I need to be"

Breathe in.
Let it go.

Relax your attention from the breath and invite some self-compassion and love into this creative space. Practice non-judgment and acceptance. There is no right or wrong way, just enjoy the process.

Repeat with me out loud:

> *"Today, I give myself permission to create. I am clearing my mind and opening my heart for creativity."*

> *Breathing in deeply,*
> *And letting it all go.*

Let's begin.

DIRECTIVE: MIND-HEART CONNECTION

1. Draw a symbol to represent your mind on one side of the paper
2. On the opposite side, draw a symbol to represent your heart.
3. What colors and images come up for you when thinking about your heart? Fill in and around your heart symbol with colors shapes and lines
4. What comes up for you when thinking about your mind? Fill in and around your mind symbol with colors, shapes, and lines
5. Now draw a bridge to connect the two together. What does the bridge look like? What materials is it made

of? What happens in the middle of the bridge? How can you connect the two together in your own life?

SUPPLIES OF YOUR CHOICE:

- Piece of paper
- Crayons
- Colored pencils
- Markers, or any drawing utensils you want to use

PROCESS QUESTIONS:

1. Do you tend to be more connected to your heart, your head, or both?
2. Which part of the image came more naturally for you?
3. How can you find balance between your mind and heart in your own life?
4. Did you face any resistance during this exercise?
5. Was there a point of celebration when creating this piece?
6. How are you feeling after creating?
7. How was this experience?

42

PROTECTION

INTENTION:

Todays meditation will focus on creating a safe space in your mind. Find a comfortable position, one that is free from distraction where you can feel comfortable to relax. Just allow yourself this time to steady your mind and calm your body.

Take a deep breath in, holding for five.
And slowly exhale.

Turn your awareness to your breathing, to the gentle inhale and exhale of your breath. Each breath in, filling you with confidence, and each breath out, making you feel more at ease.

Breathing in deeply,
And letting it all go.

Begin to think of every muscle in your body relaxing. Breathe gentle, easy breaths. Focus on the air coming in and going out. Let go of anything that you have been holding onto from the day, and enter into the present moment.

Only this moment exists.

Become aware of your heart beating in the center of your chest. Feel your pulse in other areas of your body, and come to notice how alive you are, how relaxed you have become.

Breathe in deeply.
And let it all go.

Let's introduce our centering thought for this meditation, "My body is whole, my body is safe, my body is beautiful. My body is whole, my body is safe, my body is beautiful."

Breathing in deeply
And letting it all go

"My body is whole, my body is safe, my body is beautiful."
Love yourself for who you are, release judgement, negativity, and have love and respect for your being.
"My body is whole, my body is safe, my body is beautiful."

Inhale.
And exhale it all out.

Invite some intention before your art making. Allow yourself to take the time to turn inward and to connect with your creativity. You deserve it.

As you create, practice non-judgment and acceptance. There is no right or wrong way to embark on the creative journey, just enjoy the process and let your heart sing.

. . .

Read this out loud with me:

*"Today, I give myself permission to create. I am clearing
my mind and opening my heart for creativity."*

*Breathing in deeply one last time,
And letting it all go.*

Let's begin.

DIRECTIVE: THE WALLS WE BUILD

1. Create an image of a brick wall.
2. Think through the ways you have walls in your life
   that hinder you from letting people/emotions/ etc. in.
3. On each brick, write what makes up the wall and
   explore the emotions that come up as you create this.

SUPPLIES OF YOUR CHOICE:

- Paper
- Ruler
- Pencil
- Markers
- Colored pencils
- Crayons
- Oil pastels
- Any other supplies you choose

PROCESS QUESTIONS:

1. What are some of the walls you have in your life?
2. Are there any significant moments in your life that resulted in you building up walls?
3. Do you want to tear down any walls you have built?
4. Did you face any resistance during this exercise?
5. Was there a point of celebration when creating this piece?
6. How are you feeling?
7. How was this experience?

PART X

THERAPEUTIC ART ACTIVITIES FOR DEPRESSION

Inhale.
I have never known sweet ache like this
Where it hurts to breathe
Yet my lungs still expand
Reminding me of the beautiful song I still sing
Named "Resiliency"

Exhale.
And I have felt the numb weight
In my heavy chest
While my lungs release tight breaths
And the words they sing is
"This is not the end"

— THE TRUTH IN EACH BREATH YOU
BREATHE, KA

43

SADNESS

INTENTION:

In todays meditation we are going to sit with sadness. Get into a comfortable, seated position, gently close your eyes, and allow yourself to feel. Sometimes our sadness comes and it feels deep and rooted. It may build its home in your belly, your heart, or your mind. It may come from all of the things that we see that are unjust in the world. And maybe your heart is filled with sadness that is beyond comprehension.

Wherever sadness comes from, we often try to make it retract and go away. We try to ignore it and hope that it doesn't exist. But often we need to acknowledge it, sit with it, and hold it. We need to welcome it and say, "Thank you for the ways you have opened my eyes. Thank you for the ways you have forced me to see, to empathize, and to care. Thank you for the ways you have shown me the depths of my love.". Sometimes we need to sit with sadness and let it wash over us. Sometimes we need to ask sadness where it came from, and ask it where it wants to go. Sometimes we need to look at it head on, recognize how familiar it is, and then ask for its retreat. Just like the ocean tide, we have to ask it to ebb and flow- to greet the sadness and then release it and let it go. When it comes again we cannot fear it, we cannot ignore it, and we cannot let it bring mistrust and fear. We must acknowledge it, listen to it, and then compassionately release.

So today we are sitting with the sadness, letting it greet us, and then releasing it. It may come again as it has been with you a long time, and knows the shape of your heart, but greet it as a friend and then say goodbye.

Take a deep breath,
Exhale, and compassionately release.

Breathe in deeply,
And compassionately let it go.

Close your eyes and imagine yourself severing the ties with your sadness, and wrapping yourself in a beautiful light of love, compassion, and tenderness. Acknowledge how much your sadness has taken from you, and then focus on the beauty that still remains despite this. Time in to your resilient heart that is still beating. Despite our sadness, we are able to still see beauty in the sound of song birds, the magic of forests and blooming flowers, and the joy that comes from spending time with someone you love.

Breathe in deeply,
And let it all go.

We will now focus on our centering thought of this meditation, "There is beauty here in my life. There is joy here in my life. There is hope here in my life. There is beauty here in my life. There is joy here in my life. There is hope here in my life."

Breathe in deeply
And let it all go.

"There is beauty here in my life. There is joy here in my life. There is hope here in my life."

Focus on your breathing, coming in and going out.

Invite some intention before the art. Practice non-judgment and acceptance. There is no right or wrong way, just enjoy the process.

Read this out loud with me:

"Today, I give myself permission to create. I am clearing
my mind and opening my heart for creativity."

Breathe in deeply,
And let it all go.

Let's begin.

DIRECTIVE: MOUNTAINS AND VALLEYS

Paint a mountain or valley. The mountain represents a time when you were happy, the valley represents a time when you were sad.

SUPPLIES OF YOUR CHOICE:

- Paint of choice: acrylic/ watercolor/ tempura/ oil/ etc.
- Canvas/ paint paper
- Brushes
- Cup with water
- Palette/paper plate
- Any extra supplies to create

PROCESS QUESTIONS:

1. How was this activity for you?
2. What emotions came up when processing through the mountains and valleys in your life?
3. When have you felt most sad in your life?
4. When have you felt most happy?
5. How are you feeling at this moment?

44

GRIEF

INTENTION:

As you settle into comfortable stillness, place your hands on your knees, open up, and take a deep breath in.

Let it go.

Settle into stillness, into peace. Thank you for giving yourself permission to enter into this moment and to tend to yourself.

Breathe in.
Breathe out.

Let yourself release. Dissolve. Melt into this deeper stillness.

Breathe in.
Let it go.
Breathe it out.

Trust your heart to take you deeper. Trust the process. Let yourself unfold. Let go.

Breathe in.
Breathe out.

Even if the road in our life presents speed bumps, grief, and pain, it is all part of the journey and beauty and hope can still be found along the way.

Breathing in deeply,
And breathing out.

Take another deep breath in and relax into stillness, presence, peace. Feel yourself grounded and supported. Let's introduce todays mantra to help us stay present, "I trust the process of my journey. I trust the process of my journey."

Go deeper and deeper into stillness and breathe.

Inhale deeply,
And exhale.

"I trust the process of my journey. I trust the process of my journey."

Breathe deeply,
And release.

Shift your attention towards your body. Feel the ground beneath you, supporting, holding you, anchoring you. Feel the breath coming in and going out.

Breathing in,
And breathe it out.

Invite some intention before the art. There is no right or wrong way to create, practice non-judgment and acceptance. Just enjoy the process and let yourself create from your heart.

Read this out loud with me:

> *"Today, I give myself permission to create. I am clearing my mind and opening my heart for creativity."*
>
> *Breathing in deeply one last time,*
> *And breathe it out.*

Let's begin.

DIRECTIVE: PAINT YOUR EMOTIONS

1. Create a list of emotions you are feeling. Some common grief emotions that people feel include: sadness, despair, anxiety, guilt, anger, denial, fear, isolation, loneliness, numbness, etc.
2. Keep in mind that there can be positive emotions too, such as: joy, gratitude, and love.
3. Next, assign a color of tissue paper/paint/marker to each emotion on your list.
4. It is helpful if you create a reference key to look back at what emotions and colors correlate together.
5. Create an abstract image/collage that focuses on color to express how you are feeling

SUPPLIES OF YOUR CHOICE:

- Paper
- Tissue paper
- Paint
- Marker
- Crayons
- Oil pastel
- Chalk
- Cup with water
- Glue
- Brushes
- Palette/paper plate
- Etc.

PROCESS QUESTIONS:

1. Was this activity helpful for you to help define your emotions?
2. What were some of the main emotions you were feeling?
3. Are there any emotions you wish you could feel more of?
4. Are there any emotions you wish you could feel less of?

45

HEARTACHE

INTENTION

Healing doesn't't always mean physical healing, it often means emotional, mental, or spiritual. Our bodies have the ability to heal, and we are capable of overcoming the deepest of pains, more than we often give ourselves credit for.

Let's begin our meditation today, focusing on healing.

Find a comfortable, seated position, close your eyes, and rest your palms on your knees. Allow yourself to become open to this moment. Bring all of your awareness to your breath.

Inhale,
And exhale.

Inhaling deeply.
Exhaling slowly.

Notice your heart beating in your chest, your lungs expanding and contracting, bringing oxygen into your body, and calming you with each breath.

Inhale deeply.
And exhale, let it all go.

Bring your awareness to your face. Allow yourself to fully relax your forehead. Allow your eyes to feel heavy. Unclench your jaw. Allow your tongue to lay softly in your mouth. Slowly move your awareness down across your shoulders and towards the ground, relaxing your body along the way.

Breathing in deeply,
And exhale, let it all go.

Allow yourself to feel fully grounded. Feeling heavy in the body, but light in the heart.

Inhale.
And exhale out.

Take this moment to bring the awareness to your heart as you continue to breathe.

Deep breath in,
And exhale, let it all go.

Next, visualize a light enter into your body. Imagine it flowing from the crown of your head, down into your toes, filling each and every part of your body, healing it as this light flows. Let's introduce our centering thought, "I am healthy, I am strong, and I am healing day by day. I am healthy, I am strong, and I am healing day by day."

Breathe in deeply,
And let it all go.

"I am healthy, I am strong, and I am healing day by day. I am healthy, I am strong, and I am healing day by day."

Breathe in deeply,
And let it all go.

Focus fully on your breathing, coming in and going out. Let go of anything that you have been holding onto from the day, and enter into the present moment.

"I am healthy, I am strong, and I am healing day by day."

Breathe in deeply,
And let it all go.

Tune into this sacred, creative space, becoming fully present to the here and now. Invite some intention before your art making. Allow yourself to take the time to turn inward and to connect with your creativity.

As you create, practice non-judgment and acceptance. There is no right or wrong way to embark on the creative journey, just enjoy the process and let your heart sing.

Read this out loud with me:

"Today, I give myself permission to create. I am clearing
my mind and opening my heart for creativity."

Breathing in deeply one last time,
And letting it all go.

Let's begin.

DIRECTIVE: THE WEIGHT OF GRIEF

1. On rocks, write words/create images to describe how you are feeling in your sadness. You can also write what it is you are sad about, or use color to express the feeling.
2. Next, go on a walk, carrying the rocks to feel the tangible weight of the heartache you are carrying within you.
3. As you walk, you can choose to drop the rocks as you go. Picture how this symbolizes releasing and letting go of what is burdening you.
4. On your walk back home become present with your surroundings. What are you smelling? What are you seeing? What are you tasting? Feel the wind on your skin and through your hair. Practice being in the present moment and notice the ground beneath your feet. Express gratitude for your body carrying you home.

SUPPLIES OF YOUR CHOICE:

- Rocks (as many as you need to express how you are feeling. You can choose whatever size and shape, but remember part of the activity is to carry the rocks with you on a short walk.)
- Acrylic paint
- Paint markers
- Cup of water
- Brushes
- Paper towel
- Pallet (paper plates will work)

PROCESS QUESTIONS:

1. How was it carrying the rocks?
2. How was it letting go?
3. Were there any stones you did not want to let go of?
4. Were there any stones you were happy to release?
5. How did you feel before/after the activity?

46

LONELINESS

INTENTION:

Todays meditation is going to focus on loneliness. Wherever you are, find a comfortable seat, close your eyes, and take a few, deep breaths. Relax into your body. Relax the shoulders, unclench the jaw, and settle in. Scan the body for any tightness or tension left over from the day. Take a few, deep breaths to loosen, soften, and to release.

Take a moment to focus on the area around your heart. Place a hand there and notice the rise and fall of your breath. Notice the sensation of your clothing. See if you can feel the gentle rise and fall of the breath and the beating of your heart. As your thoughts propel you into the future, or to the past, gently bring them back to the current moment.

Now, as you breathe, see if you can turn towards the place of loneliness that you feel in this moment. Can you physically feel loneliness in your body? Where? What does it feel like? Does it have a weight? Does it have a texture? A color? A temperature? Does loneliness feel moving, or does it feel still? Breathing in kindness and gentleness. Let your breath wash over the loneliness.

Breathe in deeply.
Exhale, let it go.

Do you notice any stories that are underneath your loneliness? Stories about yourself? Perhaps, is it saying how long you will be lonely? Is it saying there is something wrong with you? Is it coming from someone in your life?

With as much gentleness as you can, imagine your loneliness as a child, young and scared. I invite you to bring a hand to your heart and say anything that is comforting to the child within you. Offer love to your loneliness and know that it is coming from a place of pain.

Breathing in deeply,
And letting it go.

For this moment, hold your attention on whatever it is you are feeling. Maybe you are feeling an overwhelming sense of longing, or the felt sense of separation, fear, or sadness. Breathe and be with these feelings, right here and right now. Opening to what is. Breathe in deeply and feel what it is that is missing. Notice your needs and do not ignore them.

Breathe in deeply,
And exhale it out.

We will introduce our grounding thought of this meditation, "I see my loneliness, I hear my pain, and I am holding space for love and compassion. I see my loneliness, I hear my pain, and I am holding space for love and compassion."

Breathe in deeply,
And let it all go.

"I see my loneliness, I hear my pain, and I am holding space for love and compassion."

Breathing in deeply,
And letting it all go, exhale.

Invite some intention before the art. Practice non-judgment and acceptance. There is no right or wrong way, just enjoy the process.

Read this with me out loud:

"Today, I give myself permission to create. I am clearing
my mind and opening my heart for creativity."

Breathing in deeply,
And exhale, let it all go.

Let's begin.

DIRECTIVE: TOGETHER

Art can be better when two work at it together. Find a partner and create something with another. You can create whatever you want!

SUPPLIES OF YOUR CHOOSING.

- Any supply you would like. The goal is to just do art with another person.

PROCESS QUESTIONS:

1. Is there anyone you would have liked to do this activity with but could not?
2. Who else can you reach out to in your moments of loneliness?

PAIN

INTENTION:

Welcome to our mediation for healing. This mediation is going to focus on the areas that we are in need of healing and love. Let's take a moment to truly feel how our hearts are doing today. Accept any emotions you have, and allow yourself to truly sit with them for a moment. Accepting ourselves as we are today is one of the only ways we can overcome and heal from whatever is bothering us. Our bodies are our vehicles to a happy life, but if we are hurting and in need of healing, our vehicle cannot function to its best ability. Today, we are going to focus on our connection to our body, mind, and soul in order to heal internal wounds. So let's begin.

Come into a comfortable, seated position, grounding our sit bones, feeling the spine nice and long, and bringing all of our awareness to our breath.

Bring a deep inhale through your nose,
And a long exhale out.

Become aware of any emotions that arise and accept them as they are.

Take a deep breath in,
and slowly let it go.

Let go of any tension in your body, and release any tension in your shoulders. Let's rest our hands gently on our knees. Again, stay with your breath.

Let's take one more deep inhalation,
And a deep exhalation.

Take a deep breath in. Feel any sensations through your body. Feel your breath bringing oxygen to your brain, to your heart, and to your cells.

Inhale,
And exhale.

Allow this clean and crisp feeling of air to energize you.

Deep breath in,
And a long exhale out.

Feel the state of relaxation come into your body. Feel all of your weight sink into the ground beneath you. Stay in this relaxed, peaceful state of mind, and slowly introduce our centering thought, " I am healthy. I am strong. Love will heal me. I am healthy. I am strong. Love will heal me. I am healthy I am strong. Love will heal me."

Breathe in deeply,
And let it all go.

"I am healthy. I am strong. Love will heal me"

Welcome yourself into this present, creative space. Treasure this moment and acknowledge that you took time to tend to your heart today.

Wrap your arms around yourself, grab your shoulders, and give yourself a squeeze. You are loved.

Breathe in deeply,
And let it all go.

Invite some intention before the art. Practice non-judgment and acceptance. There is no right or wrong way, just enjoy the process.

Inhale.
Exhale.

And speak this out loud with me:

"Today, I give myself permission to create. I am clearing
my mind and opening my heart for creativity."

Breathing in deeply one last time,
And letting it all go.

Let's begin.

DIRECTIVE: HEALING WITH CHALK

1. Using chalk, create an image outside on the ground of what is causing you pain. You can be as discreet as you would like.
2. Create how your pain feels, and any words that come to mind. Pour out your thoughts and feelings in chalk.
3. Wash away the words with water and imagine yourself letting go of whatever is burdening you.
4. In place of where the images and words of pain once were, write in its place, "It is going to be ok." Or add anything that is a comforting reminder to yourself in this time.

SUPPLIES OF YOUR CHOICE:

- Chalk
- Buckets with water
- Towel or pillow to kneel or sit on

PROCESS QUESTIONS:

1. What was it like writing what is causing you pain in chalk? What emotions came up for you?
2. What was it like washing away the chalk with water?
3. What did you write in place of what you originally wrote?
4. How do you feel after the activity?

PART XI

THERAPEUTIC ART
ACTIVITIES FOR LOVE

If you force a bud to open
No flower would be seen
And this same wisdom
Speaks in parables, rather similarly

For if you are to love
Then do not come from greed
Instead, with grace and courage
Give only wholeheartedly

— LOVE IS A VERB, KA

48

COMPASSION

INTENTION:

Step into this moment fully, abandoning self-criticism, and allow yourself to be. We are going to focus on finding compassion, love, and beauty within ourselves so that we can give to the world around us.

Many of us often feel the pressure to succeed and achieve in order to feel happy and satisfied with our lives. Although these things are wonderful in their own way, they are not the root of our happiness. True happiness can be found here within us every single day. Observing the beauty around us: the smile of a child, the autumn leaves on trees, the sound of a creek trickling by- we can find happiness in the simplest things. Once we open our eyes to the beauty and magic around us we can see the miracle of existence. In this same miracle of our human life, we can look a little closer at everyone who shares the same journey and look past our differences. We can see how we are all connected by the common thread of our humanity. We all want to be happy, healthy, and loved. Acknowledging this helps us to understand those around us, and to see how our own struggles mirror anothers. Deep down, we all have more that is connecting us than what is tearing us apart. With that said, let's begin our mediation.

Begin by siting comfortably. Close your eyes, rest your hands on your knees, and begin to bring your awareness to your breath. Inhale and exhale slowly. Relax your face, allow your eyes to feel heavy, unclench your jaw, and allow all of the tension to release out of your face and out of your shoulders, and allow yourself to feel at peace.

Breathe in deeply,
An exhale it all out.

Feel the cool air through your nose as you inhale deeply, and as you exhale, notice how the air feels warm. Notice how you feel right now. Do you notice any tension in your body? Pay close attention and with each exhale let it go.

Breathe in.
Breathe it out.

Let's slowly introduce our centering thought for the day. You can repeat this whenever your mind starts to wander, "I see the beauty in the eyes of another, we are on a shared journey together. I see beauty in the eyes of another, we are on a shared journey together."

Breathing in deeply,
And letting it all go.

"I see beauty in the eyes of another, we are on a shared journey together."

Breathing in deeply,

And letting it all go.

Invite some intention before the art. Practice non-judgment and acceptance. There is no right or wrong way, just enjoy the process.

Breathing in deeply,
And letting it all go.

Repeat out loud with me:

"Today, I give myself permission to create. I am clearing
my mind and opening my heart for creativity."

Breathing in deeply one last time,
And letting it all go.

Let's begin.

DIRECTIVE: MAKE A PRAYER FLAG

1. Take construction paper or card-stock and cut it into 5 medium sized squares, or whatever size you would like your flags to be.
2. Decorate each flag with markers, paint, crayons, etc. and write a special prayer/hope on each flag for the people in your life and yourself.
3. Take a long string and fold the tops of your flags over the string, and then staple the fold.

4. Hang your flags and let the wind blow your prayers out to the world: sending your prayers for yourself or those around you.

SUPPLIES OF YOUR CHOICE:

- Construction paper/card-stock
- Markers
- Paint
- Crayons
- String
- Stapler
- Scissors

PROCESS QUESTIONS:

1. What did you add to your flags? What are some of your prayers/hopes?
2. Was there anything you created that surprised you?
3. Did you face any resistance during this exercise?
4. Was there a point of celebration when creating this piece?
5. How are you feeling?
6. How was this experience?

49

OPENNESS

INTENTION:

As you enter into this space, pause. Release any worries and anxieties from the day and enter into the present moment.

This creative space is a gift to yourself.

Settle into a comfortable, seated position. Close your eyes and feel the sensations of your breath, in and out. As you breathe, thank yourself for showing up today.

We will begin by breathing. Place your hand over your heart and feel your chest move with your breath. Feel each beat of your heart. As you breathe, notice what you smell. Notice the coming in and going out of your nose. Fill your lungs completely, and exhale.

Inhale.
And exhale.

Place one hand over your heart and one hand over your

belly. Breathe in and imagine your heart opening and welcoming the world around you. Breathe out and imagine sending your love into the world.

Breathing in, heart opening.
Breathe out.

Even when we face challenges in this life, we are able to search and find incredible strength that we have within us. We are able to develop a deeper compassion and empathy in response to heartache. Take a deep breath in and feel the strength within you. We will set an intention to open ourselves up to hope, to courage, and to love. Repeat this mantra and centering thought, "Even when the world brings pain, I will remain open to love, to compassion, to grace. Even when the world brings pain, I will remain open to love, to compassion, to grace."

Breathe in and feel yourself open.
Breathe out, and let go of heartache.

Breathe in and feel yourself open.
Breathe out, and let go of heartache.

Next, invite some intention before the art. Practice non-judgment and acceptance. There is no right or wrong way, just enjoy the process.

Repeat out loud with me:

*"Today, I give myself permission to create. I am clearing
my mind and opening my heart for creativity."*

*Breathing in deeply one last time,
And let it all go.*

Let's Begin.

DIRECTIVE: PALMS WIDE OPEN

1. Begin by tracing your open hand on the paper
2. Using symbols, shapes, lines, and colors, on the outside of the hand create art focusing on what you want to be open to
3. On the inside of the hands create what it feels like to be open

SUPPLIES OF YOUR CHOICE:

- Paper
- Paint
- Crayons
- Markers
- Palette
- Cup with water
- Brush
- Paper towel

PROCESS QUESTIONS:

1. What feelings does the word "openness" evoke for you?
2. What would you like to be open to in your own life?
3. Did you face any resistance during this exercise?
4. Was there a point of celebration when creating this piece?
5. How are you feeling?
6. How was this experience?

KINDNESS

INTENTION:

Finding a peaceful place, settle into the present moment. Find a comfortable position, and close your eyes.

Take a deep breath in,
And let it go.

Feel the heaviness in your eyes and let your face completely relax. Let go. Surrender to this moment of peace and tranquility.

Breathe in,
And exhale, let it go.

Enter into the present space with a sense of gratitude. Continue to melt into the simple sensations of your inhalation and exhalation.

Breathing in deeply.

Exhaling, letting it all go.

There is a beautiful feeling that comes when we open ourselves to kindness, to love, to compassion. The pain, regret, disappointment, and anger is all in the past. Take this moment right now to open yourself to gratitude, to kindness, to love, and to peace.

Inhale deeply,
And let it all go.

Let your breath flow freely, do not over analyze it and try to control it, just feel it and let it flow.

Breathe in.
And breathe out.

Let yourself go deeper into this inner stillness. We will use this centering thought to go deeper into this present moment, "I let go and I open myself to kindness and to love. I let go and I open myself to kindness and to love."

Breathing in deeply,
And letting it all go.

Invite some intention before the art. Practice non-judgment and acceptance. There is no right or wrong way, just enjoy the process.

Speak out loud with me:

*"Today, I give myself permission to create. I am clearing
my mind and opening my heart for creativity."*

*Breathe in,
And let it all go.*

Let's begin.

DIRECTIVE:

1. Make something encouraging for someone else and
   then give it to them.

SUPPLIES OF YOUR CHOICE:

- Medium of your choice

PROCESS QUESTIONS:

1. What did you create for someone else?
2. Who did you create it for and why?
3. Did you face any resistance during this exercise?
4. Was there a point of celebration when creating this
   piece?
5. Check in with how you are feeling. How are you
   feeling?
6. How was this experience?

ADDITIONAL RESOURCES

If you are in need of extra support, please use the following resources:

- **Suicide and Crisis Lifeline:** 988
- **Crisis Text Line:** Text 741-741
- **National Domestic Violence Hotline:** 800-799-7233
- **National Human Trafficking Hotline:** 1 (888) 373-7888
- **American Psychological Association:** 800-374-2721
- **Therapy online:** Betterhelp.com
- **Substance Abuse Helpline:** www.samhsa.gov
- **Find an art therapist near you:** https://arttherapy.org/art-therapist-locator/

AFTERWORD

I hope you enjoyed this experience with *The Art Therapy Way: A Self-Care Guide*. I truly believe that art can bring healing to our spirits and creativity can be a gift to ourselves.

I have found when I take time to turn inwards and listen to what my heart is saying, I am able to step into the person I was created to be. I truly hope that this was the same for you and that it was an enlightening journey towards understanding the self, and that your art practice does not stop here. If you are struggling to work through any emotions that may have been brought up through these exercises, please connect to a licensed professional if you need extra support.

If you enjoyed the activities in this book and would like to share your art making, you can join me in The Art Therapy Way Facebook group to connect with others on a similar journey as well as share your creations. I look forward to seeing what you create.

Yours truly,
Kendyl Arden

BIBLIOGRAPHY

Author Gretchen Miller, M. A. (2012, November 20). *Growing abundance: The making of my gratitude tree*. creativity in motion. Retrieved July 14, 2022, from https://gretchenmiller.wordpress.com/2012/11/20/growing-abundance-the-making-of-my-gratitude-tree/

Bremner, J. D. (2006). *Traumatic stress: Effects on the brain*. Dialogues in clinical neuroscience. Retrieved July 19, 2022, from https://www.ncbi.nlm.nih.gov/pmc/articles/PMC3181836/

Carnabucci, K. (2021, June 3). *Comfort boxes are soothing antidote to anxiety and a great art project*. Healing Magazine | Subscribe for FREE Today! Retrieved July 14, 2022, from https://www.healingmagazine.org/comfort-boxes-are-soothing-antidote-to-anxiety-and-a-great-art-project/

Help us match the right therapist for you. BetterHelp. (2020). Retrieved July 19, 2022, from https://www.betterhelp.com/helpme/?utm_source=AdWords&utm_medium=Search_PPC_c&utm_term=mental%2Bhealth_p&utm_content=131449602906&network=g&placement=&target=&matchtype=p&utm_campaign=15797500300&ad_type=text&adposition=&gclid=Cj0KC QjwidSWBhDdARIsAIoTVb20VQxG1ihzD22mBwz_t5jOV8UM3Bmi L2VS6eplY64SCMD4CWfVs3QaAoqLEALw_wcB¬_found=1&gor=helpme

Home. Lifeline. (2022). Retrieved July 19, 2022, from https://988lifeline.org/?utm_source=google&utm_medium=web&utm_campaign=onebox

josh, & Instructables. (2017, November 7). *Easy, affordable, play dough!* Instructables. Retrieved July 14, 2022, from https://www.instructables.com/Easy-Affordable-Play-Dough/

Klammer, S. (n.d.). *100 art therapy exercises*. Shelley Klammer. Retrieved July 14, 2022, from https://intuitivecreativity.typepad.com/expressiveartinspira tions/100-art-therapy-exercises.html

Labowitz, A. R., Beachum, T., Willis, C., Lucia, Y. M., Johnson, K. O., Ritz, D., Darlington, G., Boyer, L.-M., Lodato, J., Jones, K. L. C., & Duncan, C. (2016).

Hilton Adolescent SBIRT. Retrieved July 14, 2022, from https://sbirt.webs. com/Creating%20through%20Grief.pdf

Master Peace Box. (n.d.). *30+ creative art therapy exercises (with pictures)*. Art Therapy Subscription Box. Retrieved July 14, 2022, from https://www. masterpeacebox.com/post/30-creative-art-therapy-exercises-with-pictures

McCarthy, M. L. (2013). *Writing therapy exercise: Make A life timeline*. Journaling For The Health Of It®. Retrieved July 14, 2022, from https://www. createwritenow.com/journal-writing-blog/bid/94651/writing-therapy-exer cise-make-a-life-timeline

McQueenie, C. (2018, January 22). *Craig McQueenie*. Mynavaticom. Retrieved July 14, 2022, from https://www.mynavati.com/seeds-of-forgiveness/

Mehlomakulu, C., Mehlomakulu, A. C. M. C., says, A. B., says, C. M., Says, D. W., says, A., & says, J. A. (2020, March 28). *Tree of strength art directive*. Creativity in Therapy. Retrieved July 14, 2022, from https://creativityintherapy.com/ 2017/04/tree-strength-art-directive/

Mental Health Resources List - Welcome to Napa. Talk space resource list. (2018). Retrieved July 19, 2022, from https://www.napahq.org/wp-content/ uploads/Talk-Space-Mental-Health-Resources.pdf

National Domestic Violence Hotline. The Hotline. (2022, June 13). Retrieved July 19, 2022, from https://www.thehotline.org/

National Human Trafficking Hotline. (2022). Retrieved July 19, 2022, from https://humantraffickinghotline.org/

Raypole, C. (2019, November 11). *How to use mala beads for meditation*. Healthline. Retrieved July 14, 2022, from https://www.healthline.com/ health/how-to-use-mala-beads#how-to-use

Smith, I. (2021, September 22). *How does trauma affect the brain? - and what it means for you*. Whole Wellness Therapy. Retrieved July 19, 2022, from https://www.wholewellnesstherapy.com/post/trauma-and-the-brain

Weber, K. (2019). *"expressive theses" - digitalcommons@lesley*. Retrieved July 19, 2022, from https://digitalcommons.lesley.edu/cgi/viewcontent.cgi?article=1136&context=expressive_theses

ABOUT THE AUTHOR

Kendyl Arden is an emerging author and this is her third book. Since a young age, Kendyl has been passionate about using the arts to help individuals heal. Kendyl has worked globally in restorative justice and art therapy settings.

Today, Kendyl is an art therapist and lives in Chicago, Illinois. Kendyl owns an art therapy organization, called Muze, which focuses on providing art therapy resources to individuals in need; this book is one of these resources and is currently being used as an art therapy curriculum for an anti-trafficking organization in Morocco.

To learn more, go to www.thearttherapyway.com

ALSO BY KENDYL ARDEN

The Art Therapy Way for Anxiety

Centered: A Beginner's Guide to the Pottery Wheel and Ceramic
Techniques

Medicine: Poems for the Brokenhearted

Heartstrings

Made in United States
Orlando, FL
21 June 2025

62297128R00138